Far Point
12 Dec 2011

tracks in snow
6·2·12 Walnut House

THE LONG, WILD SHORE

Bird and Seal Seasons on Blakeney Point

James McCallum

For Steve and Jane

Hope it brings back memories of Blakeney Point

Best wishes

James McCallum.

This image appeared on many early
Blakeney Point publications.

ISBN 978-0-9541695-5-8

First Published 2012 by Silver Brant
Greenbanks, The Street, Baconsthorpe, Holt, Norfolk NR25 6LH

Design by John Walters
www.johnwalters.co.uk

Printed by Swallowtail Print, Norwich
www.swallowtailprint.co.uk

Reproduction by Saxon Digital Services
www.saxondigitalservices.co.uk

THE LONG, WILD SHORE

Bird and Seal Seasons on Blakeney Point

James McCallum

The Lifeboat House set
behind the midsummer
colours of sea-lavender.
12th July 2011

Preface

I was born in North Norfolk and have spent most of my life there. The strong sense of affinity which I feel towards much of the region is one that has developed from an early age. This cannot be said of my relationship with Blakeney Point for I can remember my first true encounter with it as vividly as the day it happened.

My family had been given an old two-man canoe by an elderly Wells resident. It needed a few repairs but, with a little help and advice, it was made sea-worthy once again. One of its best features was a foot-operated rudder which enabled it to be manoeuvred without excessive use of paddles. It proved to be an ideal craft with which to explore the saltmarsh creeks and watch wildlife and I particularly enjoyed the sea-level views of wading birds and ducks which it afforded.

On 1st September 1993 I decided to take the canoe on a longer journey through the saltmarshes of Wells, Warham and Stiffkey, across Morston Pit to Blakeney Point. I left early in the morning on one of the biggest tides of the year and planned to return on the flowing tide the same evening. The fast-flowing marsh tides made it possible to move through some of the larger creeks at an amazingly fast and exciting pace. Once, on coming round a bend, I had to throw myself flat in order to pass safely underneath a wooden bridge that loomed ahead.

The solitude of the creeks contrasted starkly with the busy and colourful scene I encountered when I reached Blakeney Harbour. It was a mass of activity: sailing dinghies, crafts with outboard and inboard engines, several speed boats pulling water-skiers, a fishing boat and a convoy of ferry boats full of tourists. I paddled a course towards the very tip of the Point but great concentration was required if other boats were to be avoided. I paid particular attention to the sailing dinghies since they were performing erratic, high-speed changes of course when tacking into the wind. Finally I made my way across to the end of Far Point and steered out of the chaos into the slack water to the east of the tip.

Great black-backed gulls catching shore crabs

At last it was possible to relax once again. I cast my eyes back across to the busy harbour then turned to glance northwards. I was met by the most amazing spectacle; hundreds of common seals were hauled out on the bands of ochre and soft yellow-coloured sands. They seemed unbothered by all the activity in the harbour as they relaxed and dozed just out of reach of the lapping waves. Periodically clouds of silver and white gulls and a few remaining terns exploded into the pale blue sky only to settle again. A closer look at the tide-line revealed mixed flocks of wading birds roosting together and waiting for the falling tide to uncover the sand and mudflats. Their flocks followed the contours of the shingle ridges until they became lost amongst the larger grey-blue flints.

I watched spellbound. I had occasionally walked from Cley as far as the Plantation and the Lifeboat House, usually to see a 'fall' of migrant birds or a rarity that had been blown off course. As I sat there in the canoe that day gazing at Far Point I realised that I had reached the very heart of Blakeney Point, a place I hadn't in fact known after all.

I spent the remainder of the day exploring and sketching. I was both surprised and slightly embarrassed by how little I knew about a significant area of the North Norfolk coast but I was also excited by how much more there was to explore.

In the afternoon, as I waited for the tide to rise, I sat near the Lifeboat House to paint some great black-backed gulls catching shore crabs. The warden, Joe Reed, and his wife Janet were also waiting for the tide. Joe came over to see what I was doing, we chatted for some time and it was interesting to hear about his experiences of working on the Point. When the tide was high enough we said goodbye before they set off for Morston and I began the long paddle back to Wells.

The events of that day had made such a strong impression on me that I decided to apply for one of the seasonal warden posts. To my surprise and sheer delight, my application was successful and the following spring I began my first season working with the seals, terns and shorebirds of Blakeney Point. The first season proved that I had much to learn but I was captivated by the challenge of unravelling and recording the behaviour of wild creatures and this quickly formed a focus for my artwork.

I returned to work on the Point the following year and again in 1999 and 2003. Although I still make regular visits there to sketch and paint, living on site provided a continuity of observation not possible during daily visits. The paintings made during the final two years of working there form the bulk of the images in this book.

All the paintings were made outdoors and, with a few exceptions, were completed on Blakeney Point. It was always my intention that these paintings would one day appear in book form but at the end of each season they, together with my diaries, were packed away in a spare room where they remained unseen, gathering dust.

An oystercatcher beside the welcome board on the Landing Ridge. June 1999

It is now a hundred years since the National Trust took over the care of Blakeney Point and this centenary is a fitting time to produce a book celebrating its riches. When I unearthed the folders and saw the paintings again I was reminded of the good times I had spent living there, working with the birds and seals. Selecting the pictures and summarising all the observations has been a very involved but enjoyable task. I hope that through my sketches and writing it is possible to share some of my experiences of this wild and beautiful place.

James McCallum, January 2012

Common seal, kittiwake, black-headed gull and Sandwich
and common terns. A painting from my first season as a
warden and the earliest image in the book.
18th July 1994

The curious antics of a group of 'piping'
oystercatchers. A small wave breaking on the
shore adds further drama to the scene.
 Far Point, 28th April 2003

Foreword

It is not fair that someone can have the talent of James McCallum.

I regularly make the pilgrimage on the unforgiving shingle to Blakeney Point. I record all birds, butterflies and interesting plants and take photos to remind me of the uplifting, even spiritual, experience. Then I look at James's paintings and writings of his own journeys of discovery, and realise how much I miss. His powers of observation, attention to detail, yet ability to make each picture live, is a talent to be envied. The many changing moods of Blakeney Point are truly captured.

It was impossible to pick out a favourite chapter or painting – you try, and if you succeed do tell me! And if you don't, then let this book simply inspire you to make the journey too.

How the fathers of Blakeney Point, Bob Pinchen, Professor Oliver, Charles Rothschild, Sydney Long, would have loved this book. In many ways it is a tribute to their pioneering over a century ago to protect and save this magical place for the nation. Without them this book may not have been written.

Richard Porter
Cley, July 2012

Wryneck

Immature grey seals dozing, stretching and
grooming in the spring sunshine.
28th April 2010

Blakeney Point Beginnings

One hundred years ago, thanks to the foresight of some pioneering conservationists, Blakeney Point became Norfolk's first nature reserve, and one of the National Trust's earliest acquisitions. This pioneering spirit is mirrored throughout the Point's history with the reserve playing an important role in other firsts and beginnings, stretching from the foundations of ecology to early ornithology and birdwatching.

Prior to 1900, this shingle spit was the haunt of many a Victorian gunner, whose aim was collecting specimens. Much of our knowledge of the birdlife of this era has come from the gun barrels of these 'gentlemen collectors'.

A party of gentlemen from Norwich got as usual a large bag, 156 of all sorts of ages, from full grown terns to birds that could scarcely rise from the ground. I was told by a gentleman that went to the Point on the 3rd and 4th that he did not see a common tern at all during the two days.
Pashley, August 1893

By the 1880s the Point had become famous as a prime site for the collection of bird specimens, particularly those of rare birds arriving in the autumn. In 1884, two doctors from London, Fred and George Power, shot Norfolk's first barred warbler and also noted the rare 'blue-throated warbler' as the commonest small migrant. They recorded at least eighty of these bluethroats on one visit, a total barely imaginable today. The Point went on to produce two 'firsts' for Britain: a Pallas's warbler in 1896, and a yellow-breasted bunting in 1905 and one 'first' for England: an arctic warbler in 1922. Commoner birds suffered a similar fate, with large hauls of waders and wildfowl shot on successful punt gunning trips.

It wasn't only the gunners who found rich pickings on the Point. With its rich habitats, breeding birds and their eggs, local wildfowlers and longshoremen relied on the Point as a free and abundant source of food.

By the 1900s the level of exploitation by various groups had become unsustainable. The number of birds breeding on the site had declined dramatically and the need for protection had become evident.

In 1901 the Blakeney and Cley Wild Bird Protection Society employed Bob Pinchen as the first watcher. Bob, a former gunner and wildfowler, was originally employed for ten weeks each season. It wasn't until 1908, that a convalescing Professor Oliver, visiting from University College London, recognised the need for long term protection of the Point's unique and important habitats. With the help of Charles Rothschild, founder of the Wildlife Trust Movement, together with Sydney Long and funds raised by a public appeal the Point was purchased in 1912. Later that year the reserve was handed over to the National Trust, to be protected in perpetuity.

Blakeney Point was one of the National Trust's earliest acquisitions, having itself only been founded in 1895. Today the organisation is more often associated with the protection of our built heritage, but the acquisition of Blakeney Point was very much in line with the early founders' vision. Today the Trust protects over 250,000ha of land and 1,100 km of coastline, with over 30% of this land designated for its importance for nature conservation on an international scale.

Rothschild and Long went on to play major roles in ensuring that the North Norfolk Coast would remain as a largely unspoilt stretch of coastline whilst elsewhere succumbed to development.

Professor Oliver spearheaded a wealth of research on the Point, establishing an 'outdoor laboratory', which led to early studies of an array of sciences including botany, zoology, ornithology, coastal geomorphology and soil science. Oliver's understanding of the links between all these aspects helped to establish the reputation of one of his students, Arthur Tansley, as the father of British ecology. This period produced a wealth of research and reports, many of which graced early editions of scientific journals such as British Birds and the first ever edition of the Journal of Ecology. The link between Blakeney Point and UCL continues to this day, with students and lecturers still using the outdoor laboratory, and staying in the little-changed Old Lifeboat House.

An area in which one comes face to face with the operations of nature in its most dynamic forms.
Oliver c.1920

Bob Pinchen was offered 'wholetime engagement' by the Trust and continued as watcher until his retirement in 1931. 'The Ark' and 'Britannia' houseboats were the early accommodation until the Lifeboat House was purchased and converted following the war. The employment of a watcher to protect the Point was soon rewarded by increases in many of the Point's breeding birds. This was especially obvious during the 1920's. After Bob retired, Billy and Ted Eales, a father and son, watched over the Point until 1980. Ted's forty-one years as watcher are still fondly remembered by many locals, not least the teas and cakes supplied in the Lifeboat House tearoom by his wife Betty! Ted found fame further afield by using the quieter winter periods to help Anglia television's make its award-winning and ground breaking *Survival* programmes.

Ted was regularly assisted by Reggie Gaze as seasonal warden. Reggie was also a pioneering photographer who in 1947 produced, amongst other works, the photographic book Bird Sanctuary. The tradition of long-staying wardens continued with Joe Reed

taking the reins from 1981 until 2003. During this period the area of the reserve was increased to include adjacent marshland to become Blakeney National Nature Reserve. The Point also became regular host to Britain's largest Sandwich tern colony.

Whilst the early collectors recognised the Point as being the place to bag a rarity, modern ornithology also has roots there. One of the first bird ringing projects involved Blakeney Point's common terns, and early ringing studies of migratory passerines were carried out by Cley Bird Observatory. Situated alongside Cley Marshes, this stretch of coast is a magnet for migrating birds, which in the late 1940s became a Mecca for British birders. The breeding tern colonies, spectacular falls of migrating birds and a succession of rarities have ensured that Blakeney Point is a familiar name to most birdwatchers.

Few nature reserves can look back on one hundred years of data and research findings. The fluctuating fortunes of the birds breeding there are evident from these records. Prior to protection in the early 1900s, few birds managed breed on the Point, with just small colonies of common and little tern present. Increases in these species, and in waders such as oystercatcher and ringed plover, demonstrated the benefit of creating a reserve. Improved protection led to further increases in numbers over the coming decades but, despite this, there were crashes in the common tern population in the late 1970s and that of the ringed plovers in the 1990s. On the other hand, Sandwich terns, a little-known bird in Norfolk prior to 1900, began to breed in small numbers on the Point in the 1920s. This was followed by a dramatic rise in numbers in the late 1970s which has been sustained to this day. In 2011 Blakeney Point was the most important site in Britain for both Sandwich and little terns but it has less than 10% of the breeding common terns and ringed plovers it once had.

The history of the seal colonies also demonstrates the ups and downs of our wildlife populations. The tidal sands around Blakeney Point have long been popular with common seals, but even with the establishment of a nature reserve these seals were viewed as a pest by local fishing interests and their numbers controlled. In more recent decades their value as a wildlife attraction has given rise to a boom in trade for local families in the form of seal trips. The common seal population benefitted from this positive attention and, despite outbreaks of a seal distemper virus affecting their numbers, several hundred can be seen regularly through the summer months. Their numbers have, however, been exceeded in recent years by a huge increase in grey seals. The first signs of a breeding colony were first noted in 2001 and by 2011 this has grown to be one of the largest colonies in Britain.

One hundred years-on Blakeney Point remains one of the country's most important nature reserves, recognised by a raft of national and international designations. Each year the wild landscapes and wildlife of the Point attract hundreds of thousands of visitors from all over the world. The reserve continues to host scientific research, inspiring a new generation of ecologists and conservationists, and provides both employment and leisure for the people of North Norfolk.

David Wood, Blakeney Point Warden 2000 - 2011

Looking eastwards from the Lifeboat House during a marsh tide. The famous landmarks of the Watch House and the wreck of the Yankee stand out well against the hazy sky.

Introduction

Blakeney Point is a well-known landmark on the North Norfolk coast. The four mile long shingle spit protrudes into the North Sea in a west-northwest direction but on nearing its tip it curves, claw-like, back towards the land. As the Point has grown new tips have developed but the earlier ones remain as a series of finger-like ridges. These ridges echo the shape of the present day Far Point and give the end of the spit its distinctive feathered appearance.

The main shingle ridge forms the backbone of the Point and the shelter it affords has allowed a rich mosaic of habitats to develop. Extensive sand dunes, saltmarshes, tidal sands and mudflats greatly enhance the area's value to wildlife. As the spit continues to grow and change in shape so many of these habitats continue to evolve. The topography of the outer spit is particularly dynamic and changes appearance from season to season.

The two lifeboat houses. A lifeboat station was first sited on Blakeney Point over 150 years ago. The black wooden building that is now known as the 'Old Lifeboat House' was taken over by the RNLI in 1861. Its successor, the well-known blue building, was constructed in 1898.

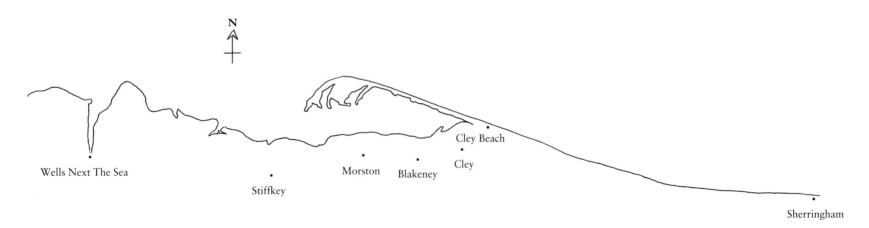

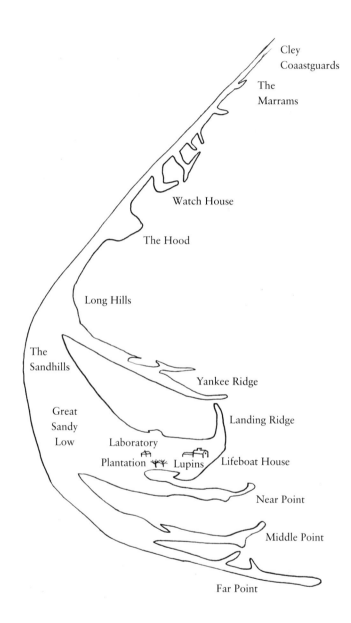

Cley Coaastguards

The Marrams

Watch House

The Hood

Long Hills

The Sandhills

Yankee Ridge

Great Sandy Low

Laboratory

Landing Ridge

Plantation   Lupins

Lifeboat House

Near Point

Middle Point

Far Point

A bird's eye view of the spit, looking eastwards. This map has been foreshortened to show many of the Point's best-known landmarks.

The Watch House was built in 1835 to monitor smuggling. It was manned by 'The Preventative Men' – the forerunners to the Customs and Excise.

Large expanses of unspoilt coastal habitats such as those found on Blakeney Point are rare and are home to many specialist species. The Point is a very important location for nesting terns and waders and hosts colonies of both common and grey seals. It is also a famous place for observing bird migration and has a long ornithological history dating from the gunners of the 19th century to today's dedicated watchers.

The following pages form a personal account of the wildlife that is found on Blakeney Point. In words and pictures I have tried to convey the changing life of each season and have taken a closer look at the lives of some its best-known species.

Spring

Early spring light – shelducks, black-headed gull,
oystercatcher and redshanks on the mudflats.
Near Point, 16th April 2003

On Blakeney Point the Sandwich tern takes the place of the swallow as the harbinger of spring. It is one of the earliest migrants from Africa to return to Britain and in most years the first ones arrive on the Point towards the end of March. The progression of winter to early spring is often erratic; dull, cold and windy days seem to bring progress to a halt but a burst of warm sun can transform the landscape, suddenly revealing that many changes are in fact underway.

Meadow pipit
display-flight

Skylarks are back on territory and ascend high into the pale blue sky in defiance of even the coldest easterly wind. Meadow Pipits put on their own aerial display when they rise above the dunes before parachuting back down with wings half-spread and tail raised. As they descend their simple notes accelerate until they become a shivering trill. Dunnocks, reed buntings, wrens and linnets complete the list of regular-nesting small birds and their songs grace the low *Suaeda* bushes, brambles and elders.

Reed bunting singing

The increasing day length and rising temperatures trigger a multitude of changes. Black-headed gulls are quick to reoccupy their nesting areas and commence their elaborate courtship displays. Each pair lays claim to a small nesting territory within the rapidly growing colonies and their collective calls are one of the dominant sounds of spring.

A sudden burst of sunlight across the open mudflats often initiates some curious behaviour in the feeding birds. Drake shelducks begin gesturing to each other by bobbing their heads in an exaggerated manner and flicking their bills up and down. The females stay close by their sides, frequently posturing at the other females by lowering their heads and angling their bills upwards. The high whistles of the drakes contrast greatly with the loud cackles of the ducks. Sometimes their displays become fevered and can result in high-speed chases across the mud or in the air. Despite the tension on the mudflats the pairs gather together in the sand dunes in the early mornings. Here they form large groups and search for suitable nest-sites inside old rabbit burrows.

Nearby, on a sandy beach, a male ringed plover calls continually as he pursues a potential mate amongst the pale rounded flints. He puffs out his chest feathers and angles his body so that his fanned tail is visible above his head.

The display of the male redshank takes a different form, a dramatic and quite beautiful song-flight above its saltmarsh territory. His double 'tu-tu' call is repeated as he rises high above the saltmarsh with stiff, flickering wing-beats. Then, with wings angled below his body, he begins a shallow glide; however, after a short descent the same stiff, flickering wing-beats propel him up and forwards once more. This flight pattern is repeated several times as the redshank scribes smooth U-shaped arcs across the sky. As the bird completes his final arc, the 'tu-tu' notes accelerate; he then begins his gliding descent and the song switches to a lovely continuous yodelling. As the redshank touches down he briefly raises his wings before concluding his display.

Skylark

A walk around the edge of the marsh shows more subtle traces of spring. A peppering of white along the dark mud of the high-water line is on closer inspection found to be a mass of tiny scurvygrass flowers. These flowers are succeeded by those of other familiar blooms such as thrift, sea campion and bird's foot trefoil which are in turn eagerly sort out by the queen bumblebees. Rising temperatures lure overwintering small tortoiseshell and peacock butterflies out of hibernation; the first butterflies to hatch from their pupae are usually the small copper and the brown argus and their colours and markings bring further life to the dunes.

The large day-flying emperor moths are sometimes mistaken for butterflies. The reddish-brown males are beautifully patterned and have a bold 'eye-spot' on each forewing. The males are fast fliers and cover large distances in their quest to find a mate so, unfortunately for the observer, seldom settle. The females are larger still and although they have similar markings to the males they are grey in colour. The newly-emerged females are much easier to observe as they remain close to the place where they have hatched. When emerging the females release pheromones which the males can detect over considerable distances. After the moths have mated this chemical is no longer released and the females then devote their energy to egg-laying.

During the second half of April common, little and arctic terns arrive; these complete the list of tern species that regularly nest on the Point. They quickly commence their courtship displays and begin to earmark potential nest-sites where they will make shallow scrapes in which to lay their eggs. Some black-headed gulls and ringed plovers may have already completed their clutches but the majority of birds are still settling down. Skylarks and meadow pipits begin to weave fine grasses together to make the linings of their nests in the dunes. Linnets prefer to add feathers and mammal fur to theirs. They have no problem finding feathers but as the search for fur could otherwise involve special trips to the mainland some of the

linnets resort to plucking fur from the corpses of hares that failed to survive the winter. The other nesting passerines can be equally inventive with their choice of nest-lining; reed buntings sometimes strip fibres from lengths of rope that have been washed above the tide-line and become brittle from salt and sun. I once found a clutch of their scribble-marked eggs in a nest lined entirely with fine strands taken from a piece of bright blue rope!

As the season progresses plant and insect life continues to grow in both number and variety and it is difficult to keep up with all the activity. Migrant birds continue to pass through in ever-increasing numbers but there are some winter visitors, such as brent geese, that

Linnets in *Suaeda*

14

seem to lack the urge to move. These birds nest on
the arctic coast of Siberia and their northern
spring arrives much later than in Britain. Their
nesting areas are ice-bound until mid-June so
they are in no rush to leave. Some brent geese
depart for their traditional staging areas, such as the
coast of Denmark, before they move on to the White Sea as the
spring creeps northwards. Many hundreds may remain in Blakeney
Harbour until the last week of May, feeding on the new growth of
the emerging saltmarsh plants. As they prepare to depart they
become increasingly restless and vocal. Eventually, one day, usually
about mid-morning, a flock begins calling excitedly then suddenly
rises in an unusually purposeful manner and heads out to sea.
Most flocks head off low over the sea in a north-easterly direction.
Sometimes there are false starts and the flock, after flying out to sea
for several minutes, turns back. However, if they continue onwards
it is possible to follow their progress until they are lost to the eye.

Common tern

The busy pace of spring barely allows time for reflection; it is
amazing to think that in a little more than six weeks the open,
desolate winter landscape has been transformed to one so full of life.
The air is alive with the calls of displaying terns, gulls and waders
and the dunes and ridges peppered with their shapes and colours.
At the height of the season more than seven thousand pairs of gulls,
terns and shorebirds may nest on the spit. Some have travelled from
as far away as South Africa and their arrival within such a relative
short space of time seems nothing less than a miracle.

Arctic and common terns fishing

Shelduck threat behaviour. The drakes rhythmically bob their heads whilst the ducks lower their necks and flick their heads upwards.
Near Point, 17th April 2003

In the early mornings scores of shelducks gather in the dunes.
There they make their nests inside old rabbit burrows.
Great Sandy Low, 24th April 2003

Shelducks regularly join forces to drive away predators.
Here a migrant marsh harrier is being escorted out of the dunes.
Early morning, 18th May 2003

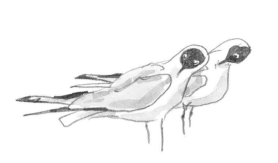

Black-headed gulls displaying

Food-begging

Black-headed and Mediterranean Gulls

Mediterranean gulls first nested on Blakeney Point in 1992. Since then the number of breeding pairs has slowly but steadily increased and in recent years over twenty pairs have nested there. Their distinctive appearance and calls are welcome additional sights and sounds of the breeding season on the Point.

Wing-stretching

Mediterranean gulls

Mediterranean gulls displaying

Black-headed gulls during the formation of their colony with several
pairs displaying in the low, soft afternoon sun.
Near Point, 18th April 1999

Small coppers nectaring and sunning themselves on the
sheltered side of the tamarisk. Strong NE winds and late
afternoon sunshine, 15th May 2003

Brown argus

Brown argus egg-laying

Emperor moths

Sea campion

Scurvygrass

Thrift with its shadows that
dance in the wind

A carpet of thrift at the Watch House

Spring Migration

Blackcaps and willow warbler. The Plantation, 16th April 2003

In addition to the important task of protecting the breeding birds another interesting aspect of working on Blakeney Point is the monitoring of migrant birds. A post-breakfast tour of the bushes to see if any migrants have arrived is one of the most enjoyable activities during the main migration periods. The first areas to be checked are the bushes immediately outside the Lifeboat House. The next port of call is the Plantation, a small fenced-off area in the dunes, enclosing a scrubby patch of white poplar, sycamore, Corsican pine and spindle. A short distance away is the Old Laboratory which has a large tamarisk on its northern side.

Sometimes the early morning searches may prove fruitless but subsequent checks in the late morning or afternoon may confirm the arrival of migrant birds. Should these arrivals be in significant numbers, and time allows, then a check is made of some of the patches of shrubby sea-blite *Suaeda vera*. These bushes, commonly referred to simply as '*Suaeda*' grow predominantly just above the high water mark and form a zone of waist-high cover. Well-trodden but indistinct paths meander through many areas of *Suaeda* and these enable the bushes to be checked without disturbing the dunnocks, reed buntings, wrens and linnets that nest there. As the variety of songbirds that nest on Blakeney Point is so limited, it is reasonable to regard birds of any other species of passerine as genuine migrants. On the mainland familiar species such as robins, goldcrests, blackbirds and chaffinches may not be easy to pick out as migrants but, on the Point, they are as obviously migrants as the willow warblers and whitethroats.

The wheatear is one of the very first migrants from Africa to reach our shores and the first males are often seen in late March. Their arrival is closely followed by chiffchaffs, sand martins and black redstarts. In early April more migrants such as blackcaps,

Ring ouzels

A white wagtail pauses to feed on flies attracted to a dozing seal

willow warblers, white wagtails and the occasional redstart may put in appearances. An explosive 'chacking' call betrays the presence of a dark thrush flashing through the dunes. As it perches briefly on top of a stunted elder, it shows a white chest-band and pale wing-panel, the hallmarks of a ring ouzel.

On Blakeney Point, as is the case elsewhere, migration is very much governed by weather conditions. A period of cold northerly winds may well halt any movement but a sudden switch to southerly winds can bring about a dramatic change. The spit is suddenly alive with the sights and sounds of migrating birds. The seven-note whistle of the whimbrel erupts from the saltings and flocks of dunlin and ringed plovers gather on the mudflats. Swallows flash westwards along the shingle ridge and high overhead the shrill calls of yellow wagtails pinpoint a small party of buttercup-coloured birds rapidly disappearing over the dunes.

Towards the end of April and in early May there is a marked increase in both the number of birds and the variety of species. House martins and the first swifts join the ever-increasing passage of swallows, and most of the summer warblers can be encountered in the bushes. The second half of May sees the arrival of some of the later species such as spotted flycatchers and garden warblers and the muted colours of the dunes and shingle can

Wheatears and willow warblers

be enlivened by the striking plumage patterns of a male whinchat or pied flycatcher. More rarely a bluethroat can be encountered and the colours of the beautiful male appear impossibly bright when seen against a backdrop of grey lichens, sand and shingle.

Male red-spotted bluethroat

By the end of May there is a marked decline in the number and variety of migrants on the Point. This period, however, has regularly produced many unusual species. Icterine warblers and rosefinches, bound for northern birch forests, may be drifted off course and carried to the Point by onshore winds. Blakeney Point has a track record of regularly attracting a small, select group of rare migrant birds at this time of year: red-throated pipits from the northern tundra and short-toed larks and subalpine warblers from the open arid landscapes of southern Europe. It is easy to see a similarity between their normal habitats and the low vegetation and sandy areas on Blakeney Point, but quite why these species repeatedly turn up, sometimes together, is one of migration's many mysteries.

Very few birds migrate during early June; late-moving reed, garden and willow warblers and the occasional whitethroat or wheatear are among the species most regularly encountered on the Point. This is,

however, the time of year when some of the rarest birds have been found: a strikingly pallid Blyth's reed warbler was seen darting after flies above the crown of some rain-soaked brambles; a booted warbler that emerged from sea fog and sang from the tops of the *Suaeda*; a trumpeter finch, pale and sandy-coloured to match its desert home picked at the thrift seed-heads with its wax-red bill; a singing desert warbler found the *Suaeda* bushes so much to its liking that it stayed for several days and was even observed nest-building!

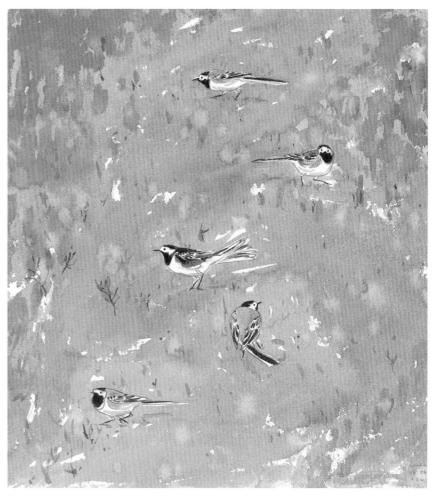

White wagtails, grounded by gales and heavy rain, join a pair of pied wagtails feeding on the Landing Ridge.
18th April 2003

Wheatears on the stern of the Yankee

Wryneck and willow warbler

Spring migrants – spotted flycatchers, redstarts and whinchats

Male redstart

Quail on the tideline

Red-throated pipit

Male subalpine warbler

A migrant redstart joins the breeding meadow pipits in mobbing a stoat.
The Lupins, 27th April 1999

16th May 2003 – A Memorable Spring 'Fall'

In spring warm winds from a south-easterly direction provide some of the best conditions to see an arrival of migrant birds on Blakeney Point. At this time of year birds often pass through quickly because they are anxious to reach their breeding grounds. Their progress is only delayed by adverse weather such as low cloud and rain.

The 16th May 2003 promised to be one such day. The morning began with a quick look at the weather outside. The kitchen of the Lifeboat House has a stable door, the top half of which blew inwards when it was unlatched. This indicated that the wind was blowing strongly from the south-east. Visibility was poor and there was a damp feel to the air. By the time breakfast was finished the cloud had already thickened and tiny droplets of rain had begun to pepper the window panes. I was joined by the other wardens and we had just enough time for a rapid tour of the bushes before we headed to the Landing Ridge to unload a boat-full of supplies due to arrive on the tide.

As ever the first area to be checked was the Lupins, a patch of mainly bramble bushes growing in the dunes beside the Lifeboat House. A few tree lupin plants are still dotted here and there but the former 'forest' that gave its name to the area has long since disappeared. On approaching the first bushes a hen blackbird shot out then disappeared from view. This was a good start but it soon became clear that this was the only migrant present. A check of the Plantation showed it to be devoid of birdlife but morale was boosted by seeing movements in the large tamarisk by the Laboratory. A russet-capped female blackcap and brightly-coloured willow warbler hopped amongst the branches. Although this was a slow

Tawny pipit

start we weren't too down-hearted as it has long been recognised that migrants can arrive on Blakeney Point throughout the day. A crackle from the radio preceded the news that the boat we were expecting had just left Morston so we set off to meet it. By mid-morning the drizzle had become persistent. With the last ferry passengers heading back to Morston and no visitors braving the walk up from Cley, we were free to have a good look around to see if any other migrant birds had arrived. A couple of wheatears had appeared outside the Lifeboat House but the Lupins still only held the same lonely blackbird.

No sooner had we reached the boardwalk, however, when a bird came bounding towards us just above the main dune ridge. Its long body and tail suggested a yellow wagtail but it appeared more heavily-built and its flight seemed to be a little faster and more purposeful. As it came closer we saw that its plumage was strikingly pale and when it emitted an explosive, sparrow-like call our suspicions that it was a tawny pipit were confirmed. It landed briefly on the bare branches of a wind- and salt-burnt elder before dropping into the dunes.

It was very flighty but, by moving slowly and trying to avoid breaking the skyline, we were rewarded with some excellent views of this rare stray. The pale sandy hues of its plumage echoed those of its usual summer home in the arid regions of Europe but it didn't look at all out of place running around the sand dunes of Blakeney Point.

Now that we had seen it well we left it feeding and set off towards the Plantation. The trees were still devoid of birds but there was now a chiffchaff and a second willow warbler in the tamarisk. Our route took us through the main dunes where we wandered through the hollows until we reached Near Point. There, another wheatear was feeding on the beach, occasionally flying onto the string fence that marked the boundary of the nesting areas. Nearby, in a large patch of *Suaeda* a handsome male whitethroat was feeding in the taller bushes. It seemed to be the only bird present but, as we approached the boardwalk, a chunky bird flew out from underneath the very last bush. It looped out over the dunes before diving into the middle of a large bramble patch. Its tail showed a hint of red which suggested a redstart but the bird was clearly larger and its flight silhouette was that of a nightingale.

Two species of nightingale have been recorded on Blakeney Point; one is the familiar songster that nests in this country and the other, the thrush nightingale, is a rare vagrant which breeds in north-east Europe. As the two species look very similar, good views would be needed if we were to be certain of its identity. Nightingales, by nature, are very shy and if disturbed they often hide in thick cover for long periods.

Since the bird had disappeared into thick brambles it seemed unlikely that it would reappear soon. So we decided to leave the area and let the bird settle down while we looked elsewhere for other migrants. On our return a thorough search of the bushes was fruitless and it appeared as if the nightingale had moved on. Disappointedly we began wandering back towards the Lifeboat House where a change into dry clothes and a hot drink would lift our spirits.

As we headed back along the boardwalk the distinctive 'V'-shaped profile of a gliding harrier briefly broke the skyline before it dropped below the dune ridge. Suddenly it came into view again and its light build and long, narrow wings with sharply-pointed tips suggested one of the smaller species of harrier. A flash of bright apricot, visible as it disappeared out of sight confirmed this impression. If it were to continue following the line of the dunes it would pass right in front of us. It seemed to take an age before it came back into view; we had hoped that it was a Montagu's harrier but when it did reappear we could see that it was something even more exciting.

The underparts were bright apricot and unstreaked and a broad, pale collar encircled its neck. The bird had all the hallmarks of a young pallid harrier, a rare visitor from the east and a species never seen before on Blakeney

Point. We watched in amazement as it glided past and headed out over the spit. It caused a brief commotion as it passed over the main ternery and was then lost from view in the low cloud and drizzle that hung over the sands of Stiffkey and Warham.

Pallid harrier

More good fortune followed that afternoon when we learned that the nightingale had been rediscovered and was thought to be a thrush nightingale. We were pleased to see it again although, for most of the time, all that was seen of it was its red tail and grey-brown back as it darted from bush to bush. Some new tactics were needed if we were to have some good views of it on the ground.

A small overgrown path led through the bushes to the boardwalk and this seemed to be a likely place for the bird to feed. We waited quietly, tucked up in the dunes trying to keep as dry as possible. After half an hour we had our first view, a high-speed run across the narrow path, then there was a false alarm when a shrew broke cover but ten minutes later the bird made another dash. The bird's appearances became more regular and it gradually became more relaxed. Its dashing runs were replaced by hops and bounds and finally it hopped out and froze right in the middle of the path.

Although it shared with its well-known counterpart the same shape and actions, its plumage was much dingier. However, the subtle, delicate grey markings on the face and breast combined with the large, dark, pale-rimmed eye rendered it quite attractive.

Later that evening heavy rain set in and this caused the bird to remain on the Point overnight. It was therefore no surprise to see it on the path the next morning. What did surprise me, however, was that after flying to the bramble bush, it uttered a few loud croaks and then broke into its loud, rich, fluid song.

Thrush nightingale

Sandwich Terns

Courting Sandwich terns and displaying little terns.
Far Point, 7th May 2003

Sandwich Terns with their shaggy crests and long black bills, finely tipped with yellow, are the largest of their kind to nest on Blakeney Point. Their loud, incessant calls and the constant streams of birds flighting between the colony and the fishing grounds epitomise the spring and summer. The link between the Sandwich tern and Blakeney Point seems so strong that it is easy to imagine that it is an age-old relationship. In reality it is a surprisingly recent association and one which has taken some time to become established.

Displaying pair

Sandwich terns were not recorded in the area until 1891 when a specimen came into the possession of H.N. Pashley, the famous Cley taxidermist. In the subsequent years they were seen almost annually and breeding on Blakeney Point was suspected in 1893. There was, however, no firm evidence of this until 1920 when a single nest was found. Sandwich Terns are notoriously fickle when nesting. Since this first attempt, breeding has been remarkably erratic with small colonies becoming temporarily established at various locations on the North Norfolk coast.

On Blakeney Point its status as a breeding bird has been no less erratic with wide fluctuations in numbers and many periods of complete absence. Although isolated peaks of over 1000 birds occurred in 1928-29 and again in 1945, it wasn't until 1977 that a colony of over 1700 pairs nested. Since then a regular breeding colony has become established which, at its peak, has numbered nearly 4000 pairs.

The similar habitats and remote location of Scolt Head Island, situated further west along the coast, is also attractive to nesting Sandwich terns. In most years the terns nest at both sites with the proportion nesting at each location varying from year to year. In recent times, however, the Blakeney Point colony has become the more favoured. The full history of the Sandwich tern in Norfolk makes for fascinating reading and a detailed account can be found in *The Birds of Norfolk*, while a fuller history of the Blakeney Point colony can be found in *The Birds of Blakeney Point*.

In early spring the courtship flights take place throughout the day and even at night, especially when the moon is out. 22nd April 1999

Sandwich terns are one of the earliest spring migrants to return from Africa. In most years the first birds arrive at the end of March, although when spring has come early some have even been recorded at the start of the month. Their numbers increase steadily from the beginning of April and by the middle of the month the majority of the nesting birds have usually arrived. Initially they spend much of their time fishing at sea and use the Point as a night-time roost. However, as the spring progresses they gather increasingly on the sands by day.

Most Sandwich terns are already paired when they arrive, the bond having been made while in their winter quarters in Africa or during their northward migration. On arrival at Blakeney Point they celebrate their pair bonds further with noisy displays which are now a dominant feature of the spring. The aerial display-flights of the pairs create a dramatic spectacle. They are performed either by mutual agreement or initiated by a fish-carrying male and take place during the day and sometimes even at night. This is particularly the case on moonlit nights when, if there is a back-drop of illuminated cloud, it is possible to follow their progress across the night sky.

Male with sandeel

The display begins with the two birds flying closely calling loudly as they begin their ascent with strong, rapid wing-beats. Their flight takes them on increasingly high circuits of the spit and harbour and occasionally well above the coastal villages and farmland. On fine

Wetting a fish

days they sometimes rise so high that the two tiny specks become lost from view in the spring sky. Suddenly they descend in a breathtaking gliding chase with wings angled downwards. They remain in close contact throughout this time and, as the chase gathers speed, their loud calls turn to an excited chattering. They sometimes weave from side to side or incorporate abrupt changes in direction before nearing sea-level once more.

In addition to these dramatic aerobatics the pair engages in an elegant and more intimate ground display. The birds stand side by side, facing in opposite directions. Their long, shaggy nape feathers are raised to form a spiky black crest. During this display they hold their folded wings away from their bodies which cause the long wing-tips to cross behind them like an open pair of scissors. While still adopting this dramatic posture they parade around each other in tight circles. As they pirouette, they continually move their heads from side to side as if not wishing to face each other or have eye contact. Occasionally both birds stretch their necks vertically and gently fence with their bills. As is the case with their aerial display, their ground ritual may be initiated by the arrival of the male with a fish.

In the following weeks the female prepares to lay her eggs. She will take on the lion's share of the incubation so she will need to be in good physical condition. The male responds to her need to conserve energy by bringing her fish. The distribution and abundance of suitable prey varies from season to season and in some springs the

The early stages in the formation of the colony. The
first pairs have laid their eggs and increasing numbers
of courting pairs gather around the nesting area.
Far Point, 26th May 2003

Pre-mating

male may have to fly considerable distances to find fish. Once a fish has been caught the tern holds it in the tip of its bill but if the fish has to be carried over a long distance it can become dry. In order to remedy this situation the male, on approaching his mate, flies close to the surface of the sea and dips the fish in the salty water. This makes the fish more attractive and easier to swallow. The male calls as he nears his mate who immediately adopts a hunched posture and emits a begging call. The female's food-begging behaviour is remarkably similar to that of juveniles later in the season. After the male has presented his mate with a fish the pair may display briefly but it is not long before the female begins to beg for food again and the male flies off to fish once more.

During the second half of April pairs of Sandwich terns start to cluster in large numbers on the sand and mud that adjoin their favoured breeding ridges. During this period the pirouette displays often lead to a male mounting a female's back where he may perch for several minutes, repeatedly raising his wings to aid balance. This stage of courtship may last several days before the pair finally mate. Often it is the end of the month before the first birds find the confidence to move up onto the nesting ridges and dunes; only then are they joined by the rest and the colony becomes established. During the early stages of nesting Sandwich terns are notoriously

sensitive to disturbance and prone to desert the entire breeding site if something upsets them. It is particularly important that they are carefully wardened at this time of year and disturbance kept to a minimum. Once the birds are settled, the eggs are laid and the adults become increasingly relaxed as incubation begins.

Periodically, however, the entire colony rises and wheels around in the air. Sometimes it is possible to identify the cause: a distant peregrine, buzzard or marsh harrier passing high overhead. At other times there appears to be no clear cause for the panic. This behaviour in terns, especially Sandwich terns, has long been recognised and has become known as 'a dread'.

One of the main threats to the colony is posed by foxes. Once a fox has discovered a large tern colony it will react as it infamously does when it has found a hen house full of hens. On the rare occasions when a fox has raided the Blakeney colony at night large numbers of dead terns have been found the next morning strewn all over the dunes. If such a raid were to be repeated then some intervention by man would be necessary if this important colony is to survive.

One, more rarely two, eggs are laid in a shallow scrape which the adults dig with alternate backward kicks of their legs and feet. The eggs are creamy-white and heavily blotched with black and brown and take about three and a half weeks to hatch. During the second half of the incubation period small white flecks often appear on the front of the adults' black caps. These are the first signs of the white foreheads of their winter plumage and these early stages of moult appear to be triggered by the process of incubation.

Sandwich terns regularly choose to nest close to colonies of black-headed gulls. The gulls are more effective than the terns in driving away predators but this protection comes at a price. When the eggs hatch and the terns begin to bring in fish for their young the gulls try to rob them of their catch.

The colony becomes increasingly active as more chicks
hatch. Some of the adult birds are starting to moult and
are beginning to show white feathers on their foreheads.
Far Point, 14th June 2003

Above the colony black-headed gulls attempt to intercept
fish from incoming terns.   23rd June 2003

There is no need to check a calendar to work out when the first young
should have hatched; a change in the adults' behaviour provides an
instant clue. The sight of Sandwich terns carrying small fish is a sure
sign that the first chicks have hatched. As more chicks hatch more fish
is needed and soon there is a steady procession of birds arriving with
fish and leaving with empty bills.

In years when shoals of whitebait are plentiful and close to the shore,
feeding the growing young is a quick and easy matter. Many Sandwich
terns prefer greater sandeels which are most commonly found around
the extensive offshore sand-bars. Most of the Blakeney terns head off
in an easterly or north-easterly direction and are regularly seen from
the sea cliffs of north-east Norfolk as they return with these large
sandeels. Studies of radio-tracked birds have revealed that some
Sandwich terns nesting on Blakeney Point frequently make round trips
of eighty miles to find these fish. The birds need to make several such
trips each day in order to satisfy their fast-growing young. On
returning from their long fishing trips the terns have to run the gauntlet
of an army of black-headed gulls intent on intercepting their catch.

The downy chicks are tended by one parent for the first week after
hatching; they develop quickly and the parents begin to leave them
for increasingly long periods of time. Even if the adults succeed in
reaching the young with a fish they sometimes have to remain to
guard the chicks until the fish is completely swallowed. I have several
times watched a half-grown tern chick struggle to swallow a sandeel
while its parent tries to prevent a gull from grabbing the protruding
tail fin and pulling the fish out from the poor chick's gullet!

The first arctic skuas usually arrive at the beginning of July.
They quickly identify the routes used by the returning terns and
either rest on the sea or wait on the beaches to select a suitable
target. The unfortunate tern is then harassed until it is either able to
outfly the skua or is forced to relinquish its catch.

The chicks' feathers grow rapidly and they soon begin to replace the
fluffy down. Many of the larger feathered young become
increasingly restless in the confines of the nest and start to wander
around the colony. Each pair defends a tiny area around its nest and
any trespassing chicks soon receive a sharp peck to send them on
their way. Groups of young start to gather on the edges of the
colony where they spend a good deal of time flapping, stretching and
generally exercising their flight muscles. Sometimes the young
gather in large crèches. Since the adult terns can easily lose sight of
their offspring amongst the crèches, the family members stay in
contact vocally. A call from a parent arriving with a fish is
immediately recognised by its young which then bursts through the
crowd, its gape open wide, ready to receive its meal.

The parents watch over the chick until the fish is swallowed

The chick's feathers grow with each passing day and the young continue to perform their wing-strengthening exercises. A bout of vigorous flapping may suddenly lift one of the young birds off the ground and, if then caught by a sea breeze, the shocked chick may travel several feet through the air before landing in a heap on the sand. Very soon these first involuntary attempts lead to longer flapping flights.

Some of the young also begin to walk about picking up small stones, crab claws, razor shells, small sticks or other pieces of flotsam. They repeatedly pick up then drop these objects and later, when fledged, develop the skill to do this in flight. Such behaviour appears remarkably similar to fishing but since the parents seem to take no part in it these activities it would appear to be instinctive rather than copied behaviour.

The sight of their young close to fledging seems to signify to many pairs that another summer on Blakeney Point is drawing to a close. To celebrate their pair-bond many terns repeat the ceremonial displays of earlier in the year. For a brief period they once again take to the air high above the spit and harbour and perform their pirouettes on the sands. These late summer displays can sometimes cause confusion for the young; a male that has arrived with a fish, rather than offering it to his expectant young, presents it to the female. The male, still holding the fish in his bill, pirouettes with his mate, shadowed by a bewildered chick begging to be fed!

As the colony is a focus for predators the adults are keen to disperse and so reduce the danger to their young. Now that the newly-fledged young are more competent in the air they spend more time out on the tidal sands at low water. Sometimes parents returning with fish can be seen trying to lure their young away from the colony; each time the young birds attempt to take the fish, the adults fly on a short distance and the young follow with a mixture of short runs and flights. When the tide flows and the advancing waters start to cover the sand some of the young retreat to the familiar surroundings of the colony, others are guided by their parents over the channel to the sand ridges that remain exposed at high water. Soon Sandwich tern families begin to congregate there on the ridges alongside roosting waders and this is the first sign that they are ready to leave Blakeney Point.

The majority of birds depart in an easterly direction; this seems natural as this is the direction which most of the adults take when they head off

A chick tries to swallow a large sandeel as the parent fends off the gulls

to fish. Pairs, when successful, usually fledge a single young but, in years when fish have been especially abundant, some may raise a second young. After dispersal the young birds are seen mainly in the company of one of their parents and they call continually to each other in order to stay in contact; the familiar 'krick' of the adults is answered instantly by the high, bleating calls of the young. Sometimes the young birds are able to fish for themselves but they generally appear more dependent than young common and little terns.

The adults continue to tend to their young during migration, leading them through the English Channel, southwards on their traditional route along the Atlantic coasts of Spain and Portugal. They stop to feed wherever the fishing is good before continuing on their journey to West Africa and many spend midwinter off the coasts of southern Africa. The young birds remain in the wintering areas for their first summer and may not return to their place of birth on Blakeney Point until they are at least two years old. The adults begin to leave southern Africa in the New Year. They spend a month or so fishing off the coast of West Africa where the pairs begin to form once again; by March many are on their way north along the coasts of Western Europe en route to Blakeney Point.

As the tern chicks grow they require more and more fish
and the increasing efforts of the adults to meet this need
becomes a focus for the black-headed gulls.
Far Point, 21st June 2003

As the summer progresses the fish-carrying terns also attract the attention of arctic skuas. These pirates continually harass the terns in the hope that they will release their catch. In this instance one of the skuas has even resorted to grabbing the tern's wingtip in its bill but the tern still refuses to give up its fish.
Long Hills, 23rd July 2003

4.07.03
Far Point, creche;
still overcast + threat of rain

As the young grow they habitually flap and stretch their
wings to exercise their flight muscles.
Far Point, 4th July 2003

Pair display while young begs for food.
8·7·03
Far Point

For a short period towards the end of the breeding season, the
adults recommence their courtship displays. The male arrives
with a fish and instead of feeding its young he presents it to his
mate. The pair perform their pirouette display shadowed by
their confused, food-begging offspring.
Far Point, 8th July 2003

The first young begin to make longer flights away from the colony. Their nervous calls are repeated as they flap over the tidal sands. Their rounded wings will need to grow a little and their flight skills improve before they embark on the long journey to Africa.
13th July 2003

Some young birds repeatedly pick up, then drop, objects found on the tideline – the first signs of fishing.
Far Point, 4th July 2003

The larger feathered young devote long periods of the day to wing-stretching and exercising. Bouts of vigorous flapping frequently result in the young terns making their first short fluttering flights but with each day their skill and confidence grows.
Far Point, 8th July 2003

Common Seals

Common seals hauled-out on the West Sands at low tide. 21st April 2011

Two species of seal are found on Blakeney Point, the common seal and its larger cousin the grey seal. Both may be encountered throughout the year although common seals tend to be most numerous during the spring and summer, whereas the grey seals are at their highest numbers in late autumn and early winter. The two species regularly come ashore to their favourite haul-out areas: the very tip of the spit at high-tide and the sands west of the harbour mouth around low-tide.

For much of the spring and summer the tip of the Point is fenced off to protect the nesting terns and this makes it difficult to view the seals at high-tide. In addition, at low-tide, they are susceptible to human disturbance and if, approached too closely, they are forced to abandon their haul-out areas and seek the safety of the open sea.

By far the best way to watch the seals is aboard one of the seal boats from Morston. The ferrymen have years of experience and know all the reliable places to find them during the various stages of the tide. The seals are so used to the daily comings and goings of the ferries that they allow them to approach closely; so much so that some dozing seals don't even stir as a line of boats draws alongside. It is interesting to observe how wary the seals have become of any noises or movements that interrupt this daily pattern. For example, an unfamiliar engine noise or the sudden flapping of a sail sometimes causes alarm and the flashing paddles of a kayak often send the entire group panicking into the water.

The two species are frequently found together at the haul-out sites and it is sometimes difficult for an observer unfamiliar with seals to separate the two. When compared to the common seals, grey seals are often larger and bulkier. It is easy to recognise mature male or 'bull' grey seals and, with a little practice, separating the adult common seals from the female grey seals is relatively straightforward. Immature grey seals can, however, be smaller than adult common seals so this can create difficulties in separating them by size.

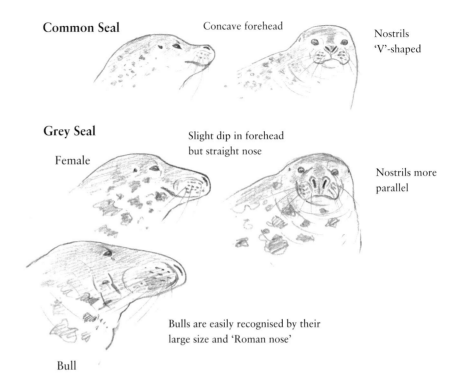

Common Seal Concave forehead Nostrils 'V'-shaped

Grey Seal Slight dip in forehead but straight nose

Female Nostrils more parallel

Bulls are easily recognised by their large size and 'Roman nose'

Bull

Two features, the shape of the head and the angle of the nostrils, are very useful field-marks when trying to identify the correct species. The Latin names of the two species also reflect their differing appearances. The common seal *Phoca vitulina* meaning 'calf-like seal' is more flattering than the grey seal's Latin name *Halichoerus grypus* meaning 'hook-nosed sea pig'.

In former years the common seal was indeed the commoner seal on Blakeney Point but, in 1988 the deadly phocine distemper virus devastated the population there and within a few months the colony had been halved in size. A further outbreak occurred in 2002 and the numbers have been slow to recover. In contrast the grey seal population on Blakeney Point has increased dramatically and it is now the commoner species.

In the literature the pupping season is frequently quoted as starting in June and finishing in mid-July but, on the Point, the first pups usually appear towards the end of this period. This suggests that either the pupping season on the Point is genuinely later than in other colonies or that very small pups, accompanied by their mothers have moved from elsewhere.

Common seal pups are born at a more advanced stage of development than the grey seals; and indeed many of the world's seal species. Common seals' first or 'baby' coat is shed whilst the pup is still in the womb and is later expelled with the placenta following birth. They are already in their first adult coat and are able to swim shortly after birth. They do, however, remain completely dependent on their mothers for the first few weeks of their lives and mother and pup remain in close contact during this period.

Seal milk is incredibly rich in fat and the pups nearly double in weight in their first fortnight. Producing such rich milk puts much strain on the mother and they can lose a large amount of weight before the pups are weaned. Towards the end of the weaning period the mothers leave their pups for increasingly long periods and head out to fish in order to build themselves up again. Ovulation takes place at about this time but courtship in common seals is seldom witnessed on the Point so it is likely that it occurs at sea.

Seals have a remarkable reproductive cycle. The egg, once fertilised, does not immediately implant in the uterus but instead floats free in a dormant state for two to three months. This 'delayed implantation' means that the females don't become pregnant immediately. The pups are therefore born at the same time each year and the common seal's annual cycle is maintained.

After the pups are born adult common seals undergo a complete moult. Whilst moulting they spend more time out of the water than they do at any other time of year. They shed their coats gradually and the first signs of the moult usually appear on the face, the base of the hind flippers and on the rear flanks. The moulting season extends from mid-July and continues until mid-September. The peak

period is August and it is at this the time of year when the highest numbers of common seals are recorded on Blakeney Point.

The hauled-out groups are especially interesting to watch at this time of year as they are continually scratching and grooming themselves. They adopt all manner of strange positions in their desperate attempts to reach an annoying itch. Once the moult is completed the seals spend progressively less time hauled-out and more time fishing out at sea. By October most of the common seals have dispersed and for the remainder of the year the Point is dominated by their larger cousin, the grey seal.

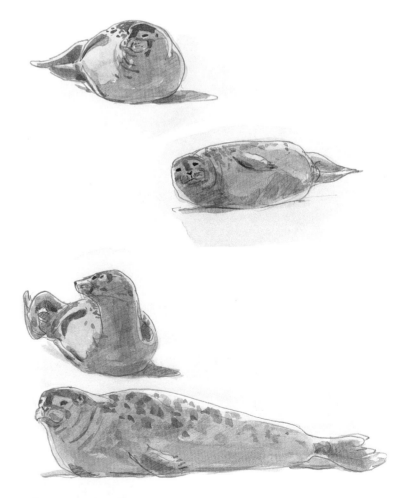

Common seal studies

Common seal pups

51

Common seal adults hauled-out

Hauled-out common seals and a fast-flowing tide. Some of the group were clearly
enjoying their basking for as the rising water lapped over them they visibly flinched
and raised their heads and hind flippers high into the air.
Far Point, 21st April 2011

A group of inquisitive common seals en route to their haul-out site
pause to watch me as I stand at the water's edge making sketches.
Far Point, 8th May 2011

Immature common seals   14th February 2001

Scratching

Ringed Plovers

A female ringed plover incubating.   Far Point, 6th May 2003

The male performs his song-flight over
his nesting and feeding areas.
Far Point, 7th May 2003

The ringed plover is a familiar bird of the shore. Its characteristic behaviour of running about the shingle beaches is no doubt the origin of its local name 'stonerunner'.

Early in the spring the males begin to attract mates and to stake claims to nesting territories. They perform an eye-catching display-flight that serves as both a threat to rival males and an advertisement to potential mates. With flicking wing-beats the males rock from side to side as they perform their song-flights over their feeding grounds and above possible nest-sites. During these flights the males sing their wonderful song, a mechanical whirring sound which, at close quarters, has a strange pulsating quality.

The ground courtship is just as exciting to watch; the male, with his chest feathers puffed out, tilts his body forwards and fans his tail before pursuing a female over the beaches and mudflats.

The male takes the courtship display a stage further when he makes a series of scrapes in the sand or shingle. He advertises to a female the whereabouts of one of these by calling to her before dropping into the depression and making scraping actions with his legs. If a female

The male displays to the female as she inspects one of his nest-scrapes

is sufficiently interested she may run over to inspect the male's work; should this happen the male will rise to allow her to take his place in the scrape. The triumphant male postures beside her with his patterned tail fully fanned and spread over her back. This attractive display is repeated each time the female inspects one of his nest-scrapes until she finally chooses one in which to lay her eggs.

The mating ritual also involves much exciting posturing. It begins when the male runs towards the female at high speed but stops just short of her. He then tilts his body backwards and stretches his neck upwards before approaching her with wildly exaggerated steps. This bizarre 'goose-stepping' reaches a climax when the male strikes the female's back with one of his feet. If she is ready to mate she will crouch down and allow him to mount her. The pair remain in this position for a few seconds until the male suddenly raises his wings, reaches forwards to seize the female's nape feathers in his bill and then the pair mate. The ritual is completed when the pair separate and run in opposite directions, the female often stopping to preen, the male repeatedly pausing to peck at the ground.

Having lost his first nest to predation a male begins to make a new scrape

Courtship Display

The following sequence of displays led to the pair mating.

1 - The male runs forwards calling with his body tilted so that his fanned tail is visible above his head.

2 - He then performs a short display-flight towards the female.

3 - The male drops into one of his nest-scrapes and begins making scraping actions with his legs. The female approaches the male.

4 - The male comes out of the scrape and moves towards the female in a bizarre 'goose-stepping' manner.

5 - The female allows the male to rise onto her back.

6 - The pair remains in this position for a few seconds until the male suddenly raises his wings, reaches forwards to seize the female's nape feathers in his bill and then the pair mate.

When the female is ready she will lay her eggs directly into the scrape. Many pairs will leave their nest-scrapes as simple bare depressions but others will line theirs with a few sprigs of dry grass, tiny stones or fragments of shell. Although the nests are usually located on open beaches some ringed plovers choose to nest on bare ground beneath *Suaeda* bushes.

The eggs of the ringed plover are pale grey or grey-brown in colour, heavily flecked with dark brown and black. They are very well camouflaged against the sand, fine shingle and pebbles. The female lays a clutch of four eggs but if the eggs or young are lost she may lay a second clutch but of fewer eggs. The eggs are laid at intervals of approximately one and a half days.

The female only sits on the first eggs for short periods in order to prevent them from becoming chilled; continuous incubation does not begin until the clutch is complete and this ensures that all the eggs hatch at the same time. This strategy is important for waders as the downy chicks need to leave the nest shortly after hatching; it would be difficult for the parents to tend mobile chicks whilst waiting for the other eggs to hatch.

The boldly-patterned plumage of the ringed plover helps to break up its outline and makes it harder to spot against the stones and shingle. When incubating this 'disruptive camouflage' works particularly well amid flints and tideline seaweed. Lifeboat House, 23rd April 1999

A full clutch of eggs. 12th June 1999

The pair shares the incubation duties and each bird develops brood-patches. These large patches of bare skin are located on the belly and allow body heat to be transferred directly to the eggs and later to the chicks. It takes about twenty-four days until the eggs hatch and the behaviour of the adult birds changes dramatically at this time. Whereas the incubating bird would have crept away when approached, the birds will now actively draw attention to themselves.

The sitting bird begins calling as it runs away from the nest, its tail fully fanned and dragging on the ground. It repeatedly spreads and waves one wing above its back before it slumps to the ground with both wings half-spread across the ground. If threatened further it moves forwards once more, fans its tail and waves a single wing pathetically above its back. Should the other bird be nearby it will join its mate in this injury-feigning tactic. This distraction display is intended to draw the attention of predators to the adult birds and away from the nest. Once an apparently injured bird has lured a

Newly-hatched young

Of all the nesting birds on the Point, the downy ringed plover chicks with their large dark eyes, pale foreheads, mottled backs and outsized legs and feet, are among some of the most attractive. They develop quickly and in a fortnight much of the down will have been replaced by feathers and the young start to look more like the adults. Young birds are able to fly when they are a little over three weeks old and soon after that they become totally independent.

During the last hundred years the breeding population on Blakeney Point has experienced a dramatic rise and fall. At the beginning of the last century fewer than twenty pairs nested there. Numbers then increased steadily and by the early 1970s had reached the remarkable total of 180 pairs. Since then their numbers have declined steeply and, in recent years, the breeding population has fallen back to fewer than twenty pairs. The cause of the recent decline is almost certainly due to predation of eggs and young. Unless this trend is reversed, these delightful birds will maintain but a tenuous foothold as a breeding species on Blakeney Point.

predator well away from its nest it quickly makes a 'miraculous recovery' and flies out of sight before creeping back to its nest.

The hatching process often takes more than two days from the first minute crack in the shell to the emergence of the chick. The young usually all hatch within a twenty-four hour period and are capable of running about as soon as their downy feathers have dried out. The parents brood them almost continuously for the first day after hatching, particularly if the weather is cold or wet.

The young are able to feed themselves and soon begin to run around and search for food. Small chicks need to be brooded regularly and so, throughout the day, the parents crouch down and call the foraging chicks back to be brooded. If the parents see danger they use a different call to tell the young to crouch and freeze. Their pale undersides are instantly hidden and their mottled brown upperparts camouflage them remarkably well against the colours and patterns of the sand and shingle. If the threat persists the adults will perform their distraction displays.

A fledged young wing-stretching

Ringed plovers are very defensive of their nesting
areas. Here several shorelarks have ventured too
close to a nest and the incubating bird rushes down
the beach to see them off.
Near Point, 3rd May 1999

As soon as the eggs begin to hatch the behaviour of
the adults changes dramatically. A pair begins to
feign injury in an attempt to draw attention to
themselves and away from their nest.
Far Point, 24th June 1999

A pair with three newly-hatched chicks feed close to a common tern
and its week-old young. The tip of Far Point, 9th July 2003

Studies of ringed plovers showing newly-hatched chicks, parents brooding and an adult feigning a broken wing.

This pair of ringed plovers had nested on a beach that was subsequently colonised by little terns. After hatching the chicks became increasingly mobile but each time they ventured near to a little tern's nest they would be attacked. Here the male, in full threat posture, attempts to lead one of the young away from the colony whilst his mate broods the rest of the chicks. The strong southwesterly wind was adding to the drama by regularly blowing small clouds of sand across the colony.

Far Point, 20th June 1999

After the breeding season ringed plovers spend much of their time in small flocks feeding on the mudflats. Their numbers are boosted by the arrival of migrant ringed plovers and at high tide they frequently roost together in large flocks. Here winter-plumaged adults and juveniles have been roosting on one of the ridges and as the tide begins to ebb the birds routinely begin to stretch and preen before flying back to feed on the freshly-exposed mud.
The main ridge close to the Watch House, 7th September 2006

Summer

Sandwich, a common and little terns bathe and preen
on a calm, bright and very hot summer's day.
Far Point, 1st August 1999

It is notoriously difficult to determine when one season ends and another begins. Not only do the seasons merge but the situation varies from area to area. On Blakeney Point summer is that short space of time between the spring and autumn migration periods; it lasts from early June to the middle of August and corresponds to the main hatching period of the terns, gulls and waders. In early June the Sandwich terns begin to bring in small fish for their newly-hatched chicks and this, for me, heralds the beginning of summer.

The behaviour of the adult birds instantly changes as their eggs begin to hatch. On the beaches and ridges the anxious calls of some of the nesting ringed plovers and oystercatchers indicates that they have chicks. While incubating, redshanks are unobtrusive but, as their young hatch, they become very vocal; the adult birds will rise into the air uttering their loud, warning cries at the slightest hint of danger. By mid-June the first black-headed gull fledglings can be seen flapping above the colony on short, rounded, wings. These first flights are an indication of just how quickly this short season is progressing.

Mottled grasshoppers and sea-heath

By the end of June some of the first fledged black-headed gulls disperse into the harbour and their places are taken by more novice fliers: other black-headed gulls and the first fledged Sandwich terns of the season.

Black-headed gull removing an egg shell

The demise of the rabbit population during the late 1990s has changed the nature of the dune flora dramatically. Formally much of this flora was grazed to a short turf but, recently, many species have started to flower in profusion: most obviously the yellow carpets of hawkbits and catsears. The spectacle is most dramatic in the early mornings or on dull days when their petals are open but, in bright sunlight they close their petals completely and the colour quickly drains from the landscape.

Some plants which are rare nationally are to be found in abundance on Blakeney Point. One such plant is matted sea-lavender which is widespread in Great Sandy Low. Here, in the heart of the dune system, its low clusters of flowers form a shimmering pale purple-blue carpet; this is succeeded in late summer by the less densely spread, deep purple flowers of rock sea-lavender. The familiar common sea-lavender is more at home on the saltmarshes where its mauve flowers dominate the upper reaches. Samphire, another well-known plant, grows along the muddy creek edges and has traditionally been harvested for its succulent green flesh. Its seeds are an important winter food for small birds such as larks, buntings and finches and also for pintail and teal.

Insects bring added interest to the summer season. Cinnabar moths fly by day and are commonly seen in the dunes; later in the summer their tiger-striped caterpillars can be seen feeding on the ragwort plants which grow there.

Butterflies bring further colour and common blues, meadow browns, gatekeepers, wall browns, graylings, dark green fritillaries and small and Essex skippers are regularly seen. Their numbers are boosted by migrants such as small tortoiseshells, painted ladies, peacocks and red admirals. The numbers of migrant butterflies fluctuate from year to year and, very occasionally, there are large influxes of a single species.

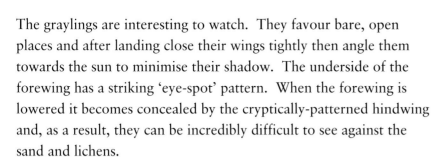

Archer's dart

The graylings are interesting to watch. They favour bare, open places and after landing close their wings tightly then angle them towards the sun to minimise their shadow. The underside of the forewing has a striking 'eye-spot' pattern. When the forewing is lowered it becomes concealed by the cryptically-patterned hindwing and, as a result, they can be incredibly difficult to see against the sand and lichens.

They also like to rest on the boardwalk where they are often joined by the fearsome-looking dune robber flies. Mottled grasshoppers also favour these bare, open areas and on hot, still days their rasping songs, combined with those of the grass-loving lesser marsh grasshoppers, are very obvious.

During the summer holidays, the number of people visiting the Point increases sharply. At this time the nesting birds are at a vulnerable stage and the wardens are kept busy reducing disturbance to an absolute minimum. Landing a boat in the wrong place or wandering

Mackerel

up to the tern colony for a closer look may seem harmless enough but this is just what the big gulls are waiting for. While the adult terns are preoccupied with mobbing an intruder the gulls seize the opportunity and make short work of any undefended young.

By the end of July many black-headed gulls and Sandwich terns will have left the Point. Successful pairs of common, arctic and little terns can be seen flying with their young but other pairs, having lost their first clutch of eggs to the tide or to predation, may be incubating a replacement clutch.

The summer months can also see large shoals of whitebait and sandeels appearing close inshore. These are pursued not only by flocks of terns but also by shoals of larger predatory fish such as mackerel and sea bass. In turn the larger fish attract the seals as well as the occasional porpoise and parties of gannets.

An abundance of small fish is always welcomed by the terns, however it is never long before their busy feeding flocks attract the attention of the first returning arctic skuas.

Even summer can occasionally produce surprise visitors such as this laughing gull from America that set up territory in 1999.

Greater sea-spurrey

Sea-bindweed

Samphire, common sea-lavender
and sea-purslane

Sea-milkwort

Puss Moths

The caterpillars of this moth can be found feeding on the white poplars during July and August. The full grown caterpillar is an impressive beast and if disturbed it will rear up to show face-like markings on its head and shoot out red streamers from the two spiked horns on its tail. If this warning is not heeded it is also capable of spraying formic acid.

A migrant pied flycatcher was seen to chance upon one of these large caterpillars. It must have thought that it had found a major prize but was soon sent packing on receipt of the larva's full defensive armoury.

When ready to pupate the larva turns purple and makes it way down from the foliage. It pupates inside a cocoon which it makes from silk and wood pulp. These remarkably tough structures can often be found low down on the tree trunks or nearby fence posts. In the following May the moths will begin to emerge. To attract a mate the females release pheromones on hatching and mating pairs are usually found close to where a female has emerged.

Unlike their larva, the moths don't have impressive defence mechanisms and instead reply on camouflage. The discovery of one of these large moths made a welcome meal for a hungry migrant golden oriole.

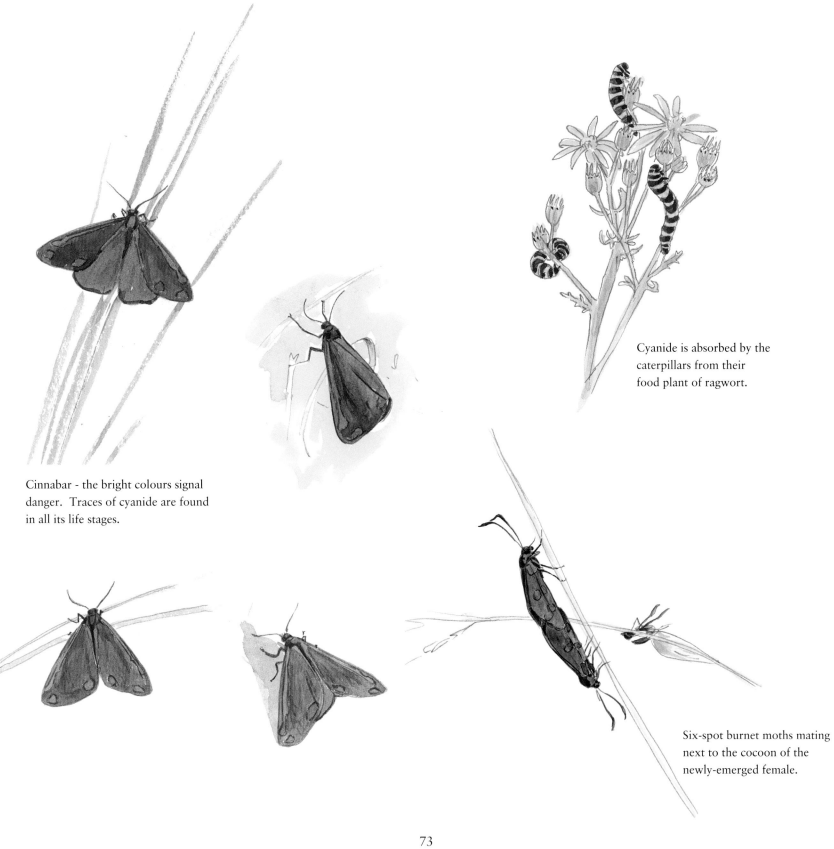

Cyanide is absorbed by the caterpillars from their food plant of ragwort.

Cinnabar - the bright colours signal danger. Traces of cyanide are found in all its life stages.

Six-spot burnet moths mating next to the cocoon of the newly-emerged female.

Small copper

Mother Shipton – this day-flying moth gets its name from the markings on its wings that are said to resemble the profile of the famous prophetess.

Male common blue

Dark green fritillary

Grayling studies

Gatekeepers nectaring on bramble blossom.
The Lupins, hot and humid, 8th August 2008

1st Aug 94. Far Point. Fulmar shearing up and down common seal colony getting extra lift from wind blown over seals bodies

A fulmar gliding back and forth along a group of hauled-out common seals.
I have watched this behaviour on several occasions during the summer
months. The sea breezes blowing against the seals' bodies appeared to give
the fulmars extra lift. This bird seemed to gain pleasure from continually
cruising back and forth and the seals watched its progress with curiosity.
Far Point, 1st August 1994

A 'feeding frenzy' of gulls and terns are attracted to shoals of whitebait and
sandeels that have been trapped in shallow pools by the falling tide.
Far Point, 10th July 1995

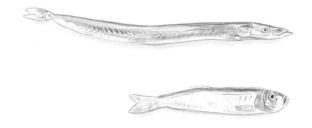

Lesser sandeel and whitebait

A large group of mixed terns and gulls diving for trapped whitebait and sandeels.
Far Point, 20th May 1995

Little Terns

Little terns incubating their eggs. The birds squint in order to
stop wind-blown sand from getting into their eyes. Their bold
black head markings help to break up their outline and their
pale grey backs blend in well with the rounded flints.
Far Point, 10th June 1999

The little tern is by far the smallest of the breeding terns. The adult birds differ further from their larger relatives in that they have yellow bills with a small black tip and a neat white patch on their foreheads. Their small size, lively character and chattering calls are all endearing qualities of this much-loved coastal bird.

Little tern preening

The history of the little tern as a breeding species on Blakeney Point has been one of wide variation in both numbers and choice of nesting areas. On the whole they are less site-faithful than other nesting terns and readily establish new nesting areas on recently formed ridges. They also respond to changes in the availability of fish and may choose to nest closer to better fishing areas further along the coast. In recent times the number of breeding pairs on Blakeney Point has ranged widely between 50 and 150 pairs but, in good seasons there have been in excess of 200 pairs.

Little terns spend the winter on the West African coast and the first birds to return to Blakeney Point arrive around the third week of April. Newly-arrived birds are usually seen resting quietly on sand bars near Far Point or fishing in the harbour mouth. As additional birds arrive they become more conspicuous since pairs or small groups indulge in noisy high-speed chases high over the spit and harbour.

Despite their small size little terns are hardy birds and strong fliers. They tend to fish close inshore and especially favour the sea around the breakers where they search for whitebait, sandeels and invertebrates. They often work a beat over the shallow sands of the harbour, fishing for sandeels, or search for gobies along creek edges. In direct flight their fast, flicking wing-beats and jerky actions can be difficult to follow until they suddenly rise and pause to hover. On locating prey the terns cease hovering and hold their wings high above their backs. They maintain this angelic pose as they drop vertically, plunge headfirst into the water and, if successful, surface with their catch.

I have often been sitting quietly by a creek edge when one of these little sprite-like birds has suddenly appeared, hovered right in front of me then danced off along the water's edge. There is no doubt that these are the qualities that inspired Ian Wallace, the great birdwatcher, to refer to them as 'fairies' during a boat trip to see the seals.

Little terns are fickle and notoriously erratic in their choice of breeding areas. They favour flat, open beaches where they nest in loose colonies on low ridges of sand and shingle. Unfortunately many of the most suitable nesting areas are on those beaches most popular with tourists. Little terns make things even more difficult for themselves by nesting just above the high-water mark and so leaving their nests vulnerable to the highest tides and storm surges. Nesting areas can be fenced off and wardened but, in spite of this, the terns are still at the mercy of the elements.

After the first birds have arrived the numbers build up quickly, the males begin displaying and pairs commence their courtship flights. The male instigates the courtship flight by bringing in a fish and

Preening individual flight feathers

Little Tern Courtship

The female greets the arrival of her fish-bearing mate with a chick-like posture and begging call.

In the early stages of courtship the male, after presenting his mate with a fish, postures in this upright manner before departing.

When ready to mate the female crouches with her wings slightly parted. Often the feathers of her underwing coverts can be seen to be raised. The male stands next to her with his wings half-spread and his tail cocked. He nervously twitches his wings and repeatedly turns his head from side to side.

Once ready the female allows the male to rise upon her back. She then takes the fish and the pair mate.

calling to the female to join him. The female then pursues the male and, with rapid wing beats and loud chattering calls they fly in wide and increasingly high circuits of the Point. When they have reached a great height the male, still holding the fish, suddenly stalls and, with his wings raised in a steep 'V', begins to glide downwards. The female immediately adopts the same posture and dives after him and the chase seeing the pair spiral down in wide loops towards the shore.

Courtship displays also take place on the sands. A male, holding a fish in his bill, advertises to a female his readiness to mate. In the early stages of courtship the female shows little interest and often rejects his advances. If the male is persistent she may then become annoyed or even fly off completely. As the breeding season progresses the female gradually becomes more responsive and begins to join the male in some elaborate posturing.

Once a pair bond has been formed the female increasingly greets the arrival of her fish-bearing mate with a chick-like posture and begging call. The female needs to be in good condition prior to egg-laying and, in common with other tern species, she will conserve energy by waiting on the sands while her mate brings her fish. After the female has been fed the pair engage in further displays which lead ultimately to the pair mating.

The pair then move to the nesting area and the female wastes no time in laying her eggs in a shallow scrape in the sand. Normally two eggs are laid but in the years when fish are abundant many females will lay

An adult making a nest-scrape

a third egg. The eggs have a matt texture and are pale creamy or sandy grey in colour with a few irregular black, brown or grey blotches. The colours and patterns blend so well with the surrounding sand and shingle that they are incredibly hard to spot.

A male brings food to his incubating mate

In the early stages of nesting the female does most of the incubation and the male sustains her by regularly bringing in fish. During the later stages of incubation the pair shares the duties more evenly and will relieve each other at regular intervals. The eggs are vulnerable to the same threats of predation as the other terns and waders.

By choosing to nest so low down on open beaches, incubating little terns often have to face not only high tides but other natural hazards. During periods of dry weather and persistent winds 'sand storms' can be a problem. The adults face into the wind and sand with their eyes almost closed and try to sit it out. On rare occasions the volume of sand involved has been so great that the birds have been forced to abandon their eggs or even chicks. More rarely a summer gale has produced a mass of sea foam and billowing clouds, waist-deep, have been blown up on to the beach and engulfed the nesting areas. During these freak events many of the nesting species, not just little terns, have been forced to desert their eggs and young.

Provided all does go to plan, the chicks hatch after about twenty-one days. The downy young are a pale sandy colour with a light scattering of fine black speckles. When the chicks are motionless their colours and markings blend perfectly with their surroundings. As the young grow they become increasingly mobile and therefore more obvious to predators. In some years the beach colonies between the Hood and the Watch House have suffered heavily from predation by kestrels. The kestrels also have hungry young to feed and, once they have discovered a colony of young little terns, they return repeatedly until the food supply is exhausted.

Downy chick

With so many threats facing nesting little terns the wait for the young to fledge is always a tense period. In one particular season there were ninety near-fledged young on a small area of low-lying beach and the whole ternery was very vulnerable to a cycle of marsh tides. Each day the tides increased in height and the area of beach left exposed at high tide was reduced in size. When the highest tide was due we realised that, providing there were no strong winds, just enough sand would be left exposed to save the young from being washed away. There was huge relief when the highest tide started to ebb. The very next morning a group of immature large gulls appeared and decided to loaf there while they waited for the tide to fall. Before we realised what was happening, the gulls had discovered and eaten all ninety young apart from two that had just learnt to fly. It was heart-breaking and what made it even harder to bear was that all the young were within a few days of being able to fly.

Young little terns develop rapidly and soon begin to replace their chick down with feathers. It is remarkable that some young are capable of flight only two and a half weeks after hatching but, despite this rapid development, the little tern's nesting season is often a protracted affair. Pairs that have lost eggs or young to predation, bad weather or high tides frequently make additional nesting attempts. In late June and even early July it is common to have an influx of pairs which settle to nest. These birds are presumably failed breeders from colonies further along the coast. Occasionally a few pairs make very late nesting attempts but, by late August, the urge to migrate has become so dominant that the birds abandon these late nests.

A juvenile moulting into its first winter plumage, 17th August 1999

A large number of young can be raised but only in the rare seasons with an abundance of fish, kind weather and little predation. It is then wonderful to see the shore alive with fledglings and those pairs with three strongly-flying young in tow are the jewels in the crown.

Newly-fledged juvenile

Counting nesting little terns is always a challenge. Here
displaying, incubating and brooding birds share the same
area of beach as a brooding ringed plover and common tern.
Far Point, late afternoon, 15th June 1999

A male holding a sandeel in the tip of his bill lands beside his
mate and this triggers the opening sequence of the pair's
courtship display. In the low evening light the shadow of his
head and bill is cast across the female's back.
Far Point, 27th May 2003

A colony of little terns incubating eggs and a single
ringed plover brooding very small chicks.
Far Point, 31st May 2003

A little tern arrives to feed its three small chicks
amid the blue shadows of late evening.
Far Point, 30th June 1999

As the young grow their appetites increase so their parents start to leave
them unattended whilst they head off to fish. The young hide amongst the
stones while they wait for their parents to return. A pair of beautiful arctic
terns has also chosen to nest within the colony.
Far Point, 26th June 1999

Newly-hatched chicks lie beside a cockle shell and the moulted tertial feather of a curlew.

A half-grown but fully-feathered young hides amongst the rounded flints.

Young Little Terns

The sketches show the development of the young little terns and the presence of familiar tideline objects help to show just how small the young birds are.

A fledged juvenile rests on the tideline where it is dwarfed by the tail feather of a young herring gull and the claws of a full-grown shore crab. Close by lies the moulted shell of a tiny shore crab.

664 young common + little flyswarmed - late pm. dusk count Littles - over 700 birds 18 . 7 . 99 .

A swarm of tiny insects suddenly appeared over the colony and attracted the attention of a group of young little and common terns. The young birds had been practising 'fishing' by repeatedly picking up then dropping small stones and the arrival of the fast-moving insects helped them to fine-tune these rapidly developing skills. Far Point, 18th July 1999

The sight of the first fledged young of the season
is a greatly anticipated and welcomed moment

Fledged juveniles

Young sheltering behind tideline rubbish

Part of a group at dusk of '460' birds roosting around breeding colony.

Adult and fledged little terns and a single common tern stretching, scratching and preening. The arrival of an adult little tern with a fish causes its two young to run towards it calling loudly with their wings raised and bills wide open.   Far Point, 17th July 1999

Oystercatchers

'Piping' oystercatchers. This noisy and eye-catching display sees
two pairs running shoulder to shoulder with their necks extended
and their wide-open bills pointing towards the ground.
The Lifeboat House, 20th May 2003

The oystercatcher's bold black-and-white plumage and long carrot-coloured bill render it instantly recognisable. Despite its name it does not catch oysters, feeding mainly on cockles, mussels, Baltic tellins and marine worms such as ragworms. In Norfolk it is essentially a bird of the coast and, although a few pairs nest inland, its old name of 'sea pie' seems more fitting.

The history of the oystercatcher as a breeding bird on Blakeney Point is a somewhat chequered one. In the early 1800s oystercatchers were regarded as abundant breeding birds but their preference for commercially harvested shellfish such as cockles and mussels brought them into conflict with man and they were heavily persecuted. This persecution was so severe that at the end of the century there were no breeding birds left on Blakeney Point. In 1906, as a result of better protection, a single pair nested and this marked the start of recolonisation. At first the recovery was very slow but it gained momentum as the decades unfolded. Impressive totals of around 200 nesting pairs were recorded during the 1970s, 1980s and up until the mid-1990s. Since then numbers have again fallen and in recent years only about 100 pairs have nested on the Point.

The birds are well-known for their 'piping' display during which several calling birds run shoulder to shoulder, their necks extended and their wide-open bills pointing towards the ground. As the birds move forwards one will suddenly turn on the spot, whereupon the others follow suit and the group continues the performance in the opposite direction.

Piping also occurs in flight when oystercatchers fly close together, calling loudly, with their necks and bills held in the typical piping posture. The aerial groups often number two, three or four birds but occasionally more are seen. I once witnessed the spectacle of fourteen birds rise from a roost and begin piping. The chain of birds flew above the dunes and over the Lifeboat House making an incredible noise as they passed overhead.

A female advertises her readiness to mate

Early in the spring the males perform a much less frantic and quite beautiful 'butterfly song-flight' above their nesting grounds. The male beats his wings more slowly than in normal flight and for such a large and powerful-looking bird the action looks remarkably elegant and graceful.

Oystercatchers frequently return to the same nest-sites each year and will sometimes lay their eggs in exactly the same spot. Occasionally visitors have stumbled upon a clutch of eggs and marked the nest by placing a large ring of stones around it to prevent others treading on the eggs. These stone circles often survive from one year to the next and, early one season, a new warden asked what the various rings of stones were for. He smiled when told they were arranged to show the oystercatchers where to nest. A month later he seemed genuinely bemused to find that one of these site-faithful birds was incubating eggs right in the centre of a stone circle!

Both the male and the female are involved in making the nest-scrape. Initially they loosen the sand with their bills and complete the work by kicking out any unwanted material with their feet. Some pairs leave the nest-scrapes unlined while others decorate theirs. Pairs nesting in the dunes sometimes arrange a few dry grass stems in the scrape whereas those nesting on the beach may add a layer of tiny stones or sun-bleached cockle shells. Occasionally it is possible to find a real work of art, composed of fragments of mother of pearl which have been painstakingly collected from the tideline.

When a female is ready to mate she stands erect and raises the rear half of her body. Her white underparts are directed towards the male, who approaches slowly in a hunched posture with his bill and tail angled downwards. On reaching her the male begins to beat his wings before rising onto her back, where he continues to beat them for a short time before the pair mate. Once mated, the females usually lay three eggs, sometimes only two but rarely four. If a pair loses either its first clutch or chicks the female will lay a replacement clutch providing it is not too late in the season. Replacement clutches are usually of two eggs but sometimes only one.

Oystercatchers are long-lived birds. Their average lifespan is twelve years but there is a record of a ringed bird having lived to over forty. Studies have proved that some pairs stay together for life and, although not proven, it is likely to be true for the majority of pairs. Since they are both long-lived and site-faithful it was possible to become familiar with the personalities of some individual birds nesting on the Point.

Incubating

In 1994, during my first summer working on the Point, the warden, Joe Reed, pointed out a male oystercatcher that had mated with two separate females. The male, in the company of two females had returned to the same section of beach for at least twelve years. The two females laid their eggs in scrapes only a short distance apart. During his daily walks along the ridge Joe had observed some remarkable and highly unusual behaviour on the part of the nesting birds. Although the total number of eggs in the two scrapes remained constant, the distribution between them could vary from day to day!

Another remarkable occurrence involved an oystercatcher that returned each breeding season to the beach outside the Lifeboat House. In 1999 I spent another season working on the Point. One of the tasks of the wardens is to locate and fence off all the nests of waders found around the Lifeboat House and along the Landing Ridge. The well-camouflaged eggs, laid in open scrapes on the beach, are in serious danger of being trampled by a daily stream of ferry passengers. That season an oystercatcher appeared to be nesting on the beach close to the Lifeboat House but its eggs were proving difficult to find. Each time I came round the dunes I could see it creeping down the beach in the way that incubating birds do when they flee their nests. Despite much searching, I found a couple of scrapes but I couldn't find any eggs. After a few days the penny dropped - the bird was actually incubating three egg-sized rounded flints. I hid in the dunes and waited for the bird to return. It walked

back to the scrape and dropped onto the stones with that characteristic shuffling of all brooding birds. It regularly changed its position on the nest and even turned the 'eggs' with its bill. Later that day I told Joe what I had found. He was familiar with the bird from past seasons and had been equally puzzled when his repeated searches failed to locate any eggs. He went on to tell me that this bird had returned to the same place each year to incubate a 'clutch' of stones. I was delighted to hear that the stones had been replaced one summer by a genuine oystercatcher's egg that had been found, abandoned, outside a nest. The bird had accepted the egg immediately and succeeded in hatching the egg and rearing the chick.

Oystercatcher eggs vary in colour but tend to mirror the sandy and stony environment. They are usually heavily mottled with black and this helps to break up their outline and make them harder for aerial predators to see.

When a nest is approached the incubating bird usually crouches then runs away from the site. Once away from the nest, the bird will then mimic the action of settling down on a nest. This 'false-brooding' may take place further down the beach, out on drier mudflats or on tidal sands. Such behaviour is seldom convincing and is possibly more an anxious reaction than a deliberate attempt to confuse a predator. On Blakeney Point oystercatchers' eggs are targeted by many predators,

A full clutch of three eggs

especially stoats and common gulls. A stoat is unable to carry such large eggs in its mouth but is very adept at rolling them away using a combination of its nose and the shins of its forelegs. A common gull, on the other hand, can just manage to grasp an egg in its beak. Whenever large gulls or other aerial predators approach the nesting area oystercatchers will fly up to attack them. Calling loudly, they repeatedly dive bomb the predator or swoop upwards to attack from below. The gulls, however, are not easily deterred and while the oystercatchers are busy seeing off one gull, another may take the opportunity to raid the unprotected nest.

Stoat rolling an egg

When the eggs begin to hatch the birds become increasingly vocal and highly sensitive to the slightest movement. During my first two seasons on the Point about a dozen oystercatchers nested along the beach between the Landing Ridge and the Lifeboat House. Since the ferry passengers have to walk along this ridge to reach the Lifeboat House it was possible to observe the varying reactions of each nesting bird. One or two oystercatchers remained sitting on their nests, some ran from theirs calling angrily, others began to false-brood on the beach and a few birds feigned injury. One individual had a more fiery temperament and would attack the unsuspecting visitors. Shrieking

angrily it would fly at people, often clipping the tops of their heads with a wing or foot as it passed!

Unlike most other waders, young oystercatchers are unable to feed themselves and have to be fed continually by their parents. On the Point the parents are most commonly seen feeding their chicks small marine worms. Those pairs that choose to nest in the dunes have to fly back and forth to the feeding grounds until the young are old enough to be moved there. One such parent regularly brought small shore crabs to its nest and, when the nest-site was inspected after the young had left, it was found to be littered with crab legs and broken pieces of shell.

During the first two weeks of their lives the young are particularly vulnerable. On Far Point they are heavily predated by common, herring and lesser black-backed gulls but, on the main ridge that leads back to Cley, they are targeted by common gulls and kestrels and few young have fledged in recent years.

If the need arises chicks readily take to the water. If there is a lot of human activity the parents often call their young to encourage them to swim short distances to reach quieter feeding areas. I once saw a half-grown oystercatcher swimming across a wide creek and as I drew alongside in a boat I was surprised to see it suddenly dive then 'fly' underwater for a few metres. On resurfacing it quickly swam to the shore then ran off to hide underneath some *Suaeda* bushes.

As they develop, some young birds begin to feed themselves. Others, however, appear to be totally dependent on their parents and it is not unusual to see fully-fledged young still following the parents around, begging to be fed. If the young persist, the adults start to drive them away and they will have to quickly learn to fend for themselves if they are to survive. Independent young frequently join the feeding groups of adult birds out in the harbour where they can be recognised by their brown-tinged upperparts and dark-tipped bills. After all the trials and tribulations of the breeding season it is always satisfying to see full-grown young successfully fending for themselves.

Common gull stealing an egg

Hatching eggs – the tip of one chick's bill,
complete with the egg-tooth, is just visible.

Flying away with the eggshell
before dropping it

Walking away with the eggshell

Newly-hatched chicks

Removing the eggshell

A June storm. An incubating oystercatcher and common and arctic terns angle their bills directly into the path of the driving rain and hail. This painting was made from the shelter of a wooden hide on Near Point. At the time this was the location of the main nesting area and over three thousand pairs of both black-headed gulls and Sandwich terns were also incubating their clutches. During the height of the storm every one of the nesting birds had adopted the exact same posture and this was held until the rain and hail began to ease.

7th June 1999

The pair call loudly and feign injury in an attempt to draw
attention to themselves and away from their newly-hatched
chicks. To avoid unnecessary disturbance all sketches of eggs
and young were made rapidly whilst wardening nests during
the busy periods when the ferry passengers came ashore.
The Bay, 14th June 1999

Coming in to attack

An agitated parent hovers above ferry passengers

Calling the young to brood

A brooding bird rises to let the chicks be fed

A pair of oystercatchers with a single chick
feeding at lowtide amongst lugworm casts. One
of the adults, having caught a ragworm, washes it
then presents it to its young.
The Landing Ridge, 26th June 2003

A downy young hiding amongst stones

Wing-stretching

Ten day old chick

Fully-fledged young pestering their parents for food

Returning Waders

Dunlins with both shadows and reflections on wet sand.
Bright sun, Far Point, 15th June, 2003

For waders breeding in northern and arctic regions their summer is very short and the first returning birds can often be seen in Blakeney Harbour at the end of June or early July. The adult birds return first whereas the first juveniles do not usually appear until the end of the July. Many of the early-returning adults are still clad in their summer finery but, as the season progresses, they increasingly begin to show signs of wear and moult. In contrast, the young birds will be sporting fresh sets of neat new feathers.

Ringed plovers, curlew sandpipers, dunlins and
a turnstone gather at low tide to feed on the
mudflats and amongst the samphire plants.
The Lifeboat House, 30th July 2003

Dunlins, ringed plovers, black-headed gulls, turnstones, a bar-tailed
godwit, a curlew and a redshank feed together on mud exposed by the
falling tide. The male turnstones and the godwit look especially
beautiful in the clear early morning light.
The Lifeboat House, 17th August 2003

Turnstones in their full breeding colours. These birds are busy searching
for sandhoppers underneath channel wrack and small flints. The birds live
up to their name by repeatedly overturning stones using their chisel-shaped
bills and powerful neck muscles. Occasionally the sudden upward flick of
one of the birds' bills would send a stone flying several feet across the
beach. With the exception of the occasional quarrel, the noise of colliding
pebbles was the dominant sound of the feeding flock.
Near Point, 10th August 2007

Hares

Hares made a return to Blakeney Point during the late 1990s following an absence of over twenty years. This recolonisation is almost certainly linked to the crash of the rabbit population which began there in the mid 1990s. Myxomatosis was the cause of the crash and so far the rabbit population has shown little sign of a recovery. Prior to the virus the rabbits grazed much of the dune flora to a short turf which left little food and a shortage of ground cover to entice the non-burrowing hares to live there.

Hares are predominantly nocturnal and spend the daylight hours resting in shallow depressions in the ground called 'forms'. If disturbed from a form hares flee along their well-trodden escape routes. They know every twist and turn of these runs and race along them at great speed. Some of the runs cross tidal areas and occasionally the hares can get caught out by rising tides when they will have to jump creeks, wade or swim to reach safety.

A hare caught out by a marsh-tide

Half-grown leveret

1st sept 03
Marrams
Blakeney Point

A group of newborn leverets curled up in the
middle of a large clump of sea campion. Only
newborn young are seen together in such a way.
After a day or so the mother will separate the
leverets and tend to them individually.
The Marrams, 1st September 2003

Autumn

Migrant red admirals and a garden warbler feed on ripe blackberries.
The warbler's bill has been stained purple with the juice.
19th September 2000

The summer nesting season draws to a close and by the end of August the majority of gulls and terns have left the ridges and dispersed. A few late-nesting terns with well-grown young may still be present along with an occasional oystercatcher or ringed plover with a late brood. The purple blooms of sea-lavender give way to the autumnal reds, pinks and purples of the fleshy-leaved *Suaeda* and samphire plants.

On Blakeney Point the autumn months are dominated by bird migration. The waning days of summer are not welcomed by everybody but for those with a keen interest in birds autumn is greeted with much enthusiasm.

Redstart

In August willow warblers and wheatears are usually the first migrants to appear. Pied flycatchers are also classic August migrants and their arrival gives a strong clue that many of the birds present are of Scandinavian origin. As the month progresses the range of species rapidly increases. Whinchats, redstarts and garden warblers are amongst the 'regulars' and it is possible to chance upon scarcer wanderers such as a red-backed shrike, barred and icterine warblers or a cryptically-patterned wryneck.

September is the month when the greatest variety of species is encountered. Blackcaps, chiffchaffs, robins, lesser whitethroats and goldcrests are seen with increasing frequency as the month progresses and there is always a chance of encountering an unusual species, such as a bluethroat, a red-breasted flycatcher an ortolan bunting or great grey shrike.

The arrival of the first song thrushes is quickly followed by that of redwings, fieldfares and blackbirds while snow and Lapland buntings announce their presence with their distinctive

Great grey shrike

'teu' calls. Winds originating deep in eastern Europe or Russia can bring exciting rarities of Siberian origin, such as the boldly-marked yellow-browed warbler and chunky wagtail-sized Richard's pipit. Both species occur with surprising regularity and occasionally two yellow-browed warblers have arrived on the same day.

The latter half of September and first half of October have produced some of the most unusual records; these have included exciting eastern gems such as Pallas's grasshopper warbler, olive-backed pipit and Isabelline and pied wheatears. Much more unexpected was an extremely lost alder flycatcher from North America.

Alder flycatcher

In the second half of October, although the variety of species starts to decrease, it is possible to witness some spectacular arrivals of migrants. Late autumn storms with onshore winds, combined with rain, drizzle or fog can ground large numbers of migrant birds on the Point. Robins and goldcrests can arrive in the hundreds but it is the thrushes that dominate some of the most spectacular 'falls'.

Occasionally thousands of redwings and fieldfares and hundreds of blackbirds and song thrushes have made dramatic landfalls. On hearing their contact calls answered or on first sight of land, great numbers pour out of the gloom to seek shelter in the dunes and bushes. Some are clearly exhausted and have just enough reserves left to carry them beyond the breakers where they cower amongst the flotsam and jetsam while they regain their strength.

On such days a walk through the bushes can cause birds to erupt from every available scrap of cover, the numbers boosted by the arrival of late autumn migrants such as jack snipe and woodcock or a richly-coloured short-eared owl.

27th October 2009 - brisk SE winds with low cloud and drizzle. Huge numbers of thrushes were arriving and their calls could be continually heard high above the cloud. Fieldfares were the most numerous and during the course of the afternoon thousands were seen arriving in flocks up to seven-hundred strong. Blackbirds, redwings and song thrushes were also arriving in impressive numbers and several ring ouzels added further variety. The majority of the fieldfares and redwings passed high over the spit and continued inland. In contrast the other thrushes chose to make landfall on the Point.

Redwing

The arrival of the flocks of blackbirds was by far the most dramatic. As each group sighted land they must have literally folded their wings and plummeted down. The air rushing over each bird's body could be clearly heard and the arrival of a flock sounded like a shower of falling arrows. Nothing could be seen of the birds until the very moment they alighted on the bushes then, suddenly, there were scores of blackbirds all around me.

By early November the migration season is coming to an end but it is still possible to see some arrivals of birds. Thrushes, robins and woodcock are typical species encountered during these late autumn 'falls'. Sometimes a late chiffchaff, goldcrest or blackcap can be found in the bushes or a short-eared or long-eared owl may be seen to arrive over the sea before seeking refuge in the dunes. Onshore winds can still turn up a few surprises even at this late stage of the season. Despite the shorter day length and frequent periods of rough weather, perseverance has rewarded observers with exciting sightings of Siberian species such as red-flanked bluetail and Pallas's and dusky warblers. By the middle of the month sightings of migrant birds dwindle and the Point looks and feels increasingly wintry.

Fieldfare

Naturally, memories of autumn on Blakeney Point principally involve large 'falls' of birds or an exciting rarity and it is easy to forget the long weeks of westerly winds when not a solitary willow warbler graces the bushes or a wheatear the stony ridges. Even when there are lots of birds arriving it is not a place for the faint-hearted. The landscape is open and exposed and it requires up to twelve miles of walking, predominantly on shingle, to check all the bushes.

Looking for migrants on the Point requires different skills to those needed when birdwatching in coastal woodlands. Many birds are only seen as they flit ahead or loop around behind you. It is as useful to be able to recognise flight behaviour and silhouettes as it is colours and markings.

Short-eared owl

A good philosophy is not to build up your hopes of seeing a large 'fall' of migrants but rather to enjoy the experience of birdwatching in this unique habitat. Personally, I thoroughly enjoy the experience but it doesn't suit everyone. On more than one occasion after what I have felt was a good day I have heard a companion remark ''Never again''!

Woodcock in the Plantation

What constitutes a memorable sighting will of course vary from person to person. One of my most prized encounters involves a common migrant on a late September day.

Chiffchaff

27th September 2007, strong NNW winds with rain squalls.
During the afternoon there was a small arrival of birds which included a wave of over sixty goldcrests. I watched one of these tiny birds arrive in off the sea. It flitted over the beach, regularly sounding its high, thin 'see-see-see' call. Then, with typical bouncing flight, it skipped along the ridge towards where I was standing. Being aware that I was the highest point around, I remained silent and stood perfectly still while following the goldcrest's progress with my eyes.

It continued towards me and then, to my amazement and sheer delight, it landed on the bottom seam of my raincoat! For nearly half a minute that beautiful little creature remained clinging to the fabric, its head on one side looking up at me with one of its large dark eyes. It didn't appear particularly tired and continued to call at regular intervals.

I dared not move and watched spellbound until one of its calls was replied to and it flitted on a few yards to join another of its kind that was feeding in a thick Suaeda bush. Together they flitted about looking for insects and it seemed impossible that these tiny birds, barely three inches from bill tip to tail, had just flown through the wind and rain across the North Sea.

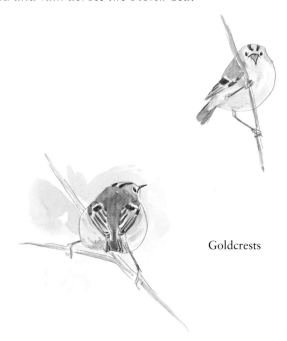

Goldcrests

Juvenile dotterels

Red-backed shrike

Wryneck feeding on ants

07 August 02 late afternoon
Blakeney Point Lupins,
Pied Flycatcher + Icterine in
Elders - sunny with light NE + mist

Young pied flycatcher and icterine warbler in a bare, stunted elder
bush - two classic early autumn drift migrants. The Lupins, sunny
but a light north east wind blowing mist in from the sea.
7th August 2002

An autumn 'fall' - redstart, whinchats, pied flycatcher, lesser whitethroat and wryneck.

Weary travellers - part of a huge influx of painted
lady butterflies that occurred in June 2003

Migrants eating migrants - spotted flycatcher and painted lady

The wonderful sight of migrant birds feeding together along
the fence of the Plantation. During the day a 'fall' of birds
had occurred as a result of strong north-northwest winds.
In the late afternoon the sun came out and swarms of insects
appeared on the sheltered side of the trees. Several pied
flycatchers, willow warblers and a young red-backed shrike
could be seen flycatching from the fence line.
28th August 2002

The sudden flash of the black and red tail of
a bluethroat is a rare and exciting moment

Pallas's grasshopper warbler

Redstart

Bluethroat

An Exciting August 'Fall'

During the peak migration periods it becomes second nature to keep a daily eye on the weather charts. Those for 21st August 2007 looked very promising for an arrival of migrant birds on Blakeney Point as there was a high pressure system over Scandinavia and northwestern Russia combined with a low pressure area over the Low Countries.

Barred warbler
breaking cover

The fine weather in the high pressure area would encourage birds to migrate and the easterly airflow would then cause some of them to be drifted westwards. On reaching the North Sea they would enter an area of strengthening northerly winds which would carry them directly to the North Norfolk coast, where the prospect of low cloud and rain meant that they were likely to be grounded on arrival.

Predicting the weather and its effect on migrant birds is notoriously difficult and past experience has taught observers not to build up their hopes for a 'fall' of birds. Nevertheless there was an air of excitement when we reached the first bushes that morning. By midday, however, very few migrant birds were in evidence and a feeling of disappointment had started to creep in.

Suddenly news reached us that a barred warbler had been found close to the Watch House. One of the wardens wandered down to look for it and, while he was watching it, an even rarer greenish warbler appeared in a neighbouring bush. This small leaf warbler breeds in the Russian taiga and its arrival suggested that the weather forecast had indeed been accurate.

With our spirits raised we set off after lunch for another tour of the bushes. A few more willow warblers were in evidence and a garden warbler and a whinchat were 'new in'. By half past two birds were turning up everywhere. Wheatears suddenly appeared on the roofs of the small huts and on fence posts. The next port of call was the Plantation. As we approached we noticed that that the spotted flycatcher that had been seen in the morning was busily chasing another one away from its favourite perches. Two pied flycatchers were flicking their wings and calling to each other. With a sudden 'whoosh' a garden warbler, its wings folded tightly, dropped like a dart out of the low cloud and landed in the poplars. It perched motionless for a minute or so regaining its strength and familiarising itself with its new surroundings.

A movement in the crown of the largest sycamore drew our eyes to a rather pale and elongated warbler. It poked its head out from behind one of the large leaves and revealed a long, pointed, pink bill and dark eye set in a rather featureless face. When the bird moved into full view its delicate lemon-washed throat, blue-grey legs and striking pale wing-panel showed it to be a young icterine warbler. This rare straggler from distant birch forests was the third rare warbler to be seen on Blakeney Point that day.

Icterine warbler

As it searched for insects amongst the sycamore leaves an explosive call rang out several times from the neighbouring poplars. Although it clearly emanated from a leaf warbler its note was remarkably similar to that of a pied wagtail. It seemed to take an age before a small bird, silver-white below, grey-green above with a striking off-white stripe above its eye flitted in to view. A thin white wing-bar and dark legs completed the picture. A second greenish warbler had arrived on the Point and was flitting through the canopy with characteristic dashing movements. In the space of an hour this small patch of shrubby trees, largely empty of birds for much of the day, had been transformed and now resembled a minute slice of Russian taiga!

Having enjoyed the spectacle at the Plantation we decided to check the *Suaeda* bushes which border Yankee Ridge. As the tide was low we were able to nip across Pinchen's Creek and begin our search at the tip of the ridge before progressing northwards along its length. More willow and garden warblers had arrived in the bushes and several wheatears were dotted over the open ground or perched on the wreck of the Yankee. A redstart, a pied flycatcher and a lesser whitethroat added further variety.

Great snipe rising from the ridge

Lesser Whitethroat

We fanned out as we approached the widest section of the ridge. I wandered along a path which was bordered irregularly with tufts of longer grass. A few wheatears flashed their black-and-white tails as they

flew ahead but my thoughts repeatedly drifted back to that wonderful hour spent at the Plantation. I was awoken from my daydreaming by a clatter of wings as a large bird exploded from almost underfoot. Its size and bulk suggested a woodcock but it had a striped back and a black bar through each wing, bordered by two white 'corporal-stripes'. It was a great snipe, so I shouted to the others as I knew that neither had seen this rare vagrant before. The bird flew towards a small area of saltmarsh, momentarily fanning its gleaming, white-edged tail as it crashed into a patch of sea-purslane and *Spartina* grass.

Keeping our eyes fixed on the spot where it had landed, we carefully approached and began scanning the vegetation but the bird's patterned feathers proved too effective a camouflage against the saltmarsh flora. Suddenly it took flight once more, uttering a couple of quiet, gruff calls on rising. It headed back over the ridge with slow, steady wing-beats before disappearing into the middle of the saltmarsh.

There was still enough light left for a wander around the outer ridges. The *Suaeda* bushes held a good variety of migrants including the day's first robin, chiffchaff, sedge warbler and yellow wagtail. A quick scan of the sea revealed an adult and a juvenile black tern lingering offshore, dip-feeding behind the breakers. Walking back along the western edge of Near Point a couple of willow warblers flitted ahead and were soon to be joined by a third warbler. This bird looked distinctly smaller and shorter-tailed. Although the bird was mobile we stalked it successfully and were rewarded with good views of another greenish warbler!

The strong northerly winds continued to blow throughout the night. Low cloud shrouded the coast with drizzle interspersed with frequent squalls of heavier rain. The next day began with an early morning seawatch. In the half-light we wound our way through the sheltered slacks to the seawatching hide. On reaching the top of the final dune ridge the skyline opened up and we were greeted by a dramatic seascape. A heavy swell was running and white wave crests stretched as far as the horizon. Out in the open the wind felt much stronger and we could taste the salt in the fine spray from the barrage of breakers that continually pounded the shore.

Inside the hide it felt pleasantly dry and sheltered. A steady stream of gannets passed eastwards and, from time to time they passed small flocks of teal hurrying westwards. More than forty arctic skuas were seen in the space of two hours. Most were on their own or in pairs but occasionally small groups passed through. The majority were adults and there was a fair mix of pale, intermediate and dark phase birds.

A single pomarine skua was picked out as it flew by just beyond the surf. It was a striking pale phase bird and its heavy build, broad-based wings and pale bill with neat black tip distinguished it from the arctic skuas. The normally diagnostic 'spoon-ended' tail-streamers were broken and had been worn down to a short thick stump.

Spotted flycatcher

Other pelagic species were less evident with only half a dozen fulmars and two Manx shearwaters picked up as they arced above the skyline. Nevertheless, there was one surprise to quicken the heart rate. As I scanned the sea my attention was drawn to a large seabird. Although it was some distance away its shape and flight actions appeared unusual. It was flying in a very controlled manner, as if untroubled by the rough weather. Its flight alternated between short periods of slow, relaxed wing beats and long arcing glides. As it flew its wings were bowed and held slightly forwards. This posture suggested Cory's shearwater, a species I had not seen for many years and never before in Britain.

As it came closer we saw it was grey-brown above with darker wingtips. The tail was short and dark and contrasted with a thin but obvious white horseshoe where it met its lower back. Sometimes, as the bird arced up, its underparts could be seen to be gleaming white except for a broad dark trailing edge to the wings.

Although the sea had provided an exciting start to the day, the events of the previous day soon drew us back to the bushes. To our delight many of the small passerines were still present and it was soon apparent that more migrants had also arrived. The was no sign of the icterine warbler in the Plantation but the greenish warbler was still there and although it even gave a short burst of song it proved quite difficult to see. However, the best entertainment was provided by an incredibly tame spotted flycatcher which would perch within a couple of feet and dart out to take small insects buzzing around our heads.

On a further visit to the Plantation during the afternoon we had good views of the greenish warbler. Then, after a very heavy rain shower, it suddenly began singing loudly and calling continually. It became very agitated and flew around the canopy in an excited manner. The reason for all the commotion soon became clear when, amazingly, it was seen in hot pursuit of an another greenish warbler which had presumably been grounded by the rain storm. At one stage the two birds, flanked by a willow warbler and spotted flycatcher, sat alongside each other on the wire boundary fence. It would have made a nice sketch but few would have thought it credible. After a while the original bird became more tolerant of the newcomer. They seemed to have come to an arrangement; the new arrival banished to the breezy northern end, while the original bird claimed its favourite sycamore and the southern clump of white poplars.

Additional new birds found that day included two reed warblers. They shot low like arrows from one patch of cover to the next showing their rusty washed rumps and long rounded tails.

Wryneck diving into cover

Wood warbler

A wryneck, flushed from underfoot, was a welcome surprise. It too was elusive and all we saw of it was an ash-grey, long-tailed bird flying away from us but its unique shape, flight manner and the dark diamond insignia set lengthways along its back made identification straightforward. We quickly realised that we were unlikely to see it well so decided to leave it in peace.

Moving onwards to the tip of Far Point we were met by a beautiful sight. A small bird shot in between some dense clumps of *Suaeda* bushes. Its upperparts appeared to be a bright golden-green and almost seemed to glow in the dull light. We carefully crept up to the last few bushes and peered behind them. There, all fluffed up, sitting on the bare sand amongst the dome-shaped bushes was a wood warbler. In the gloom its bright yellow throat and mossy-green upperparts looked more beautiful than ever. It was very confiding and, sheltered from the strong wind, seemed quite content to hop about the bare sand searching for insects.

Leaving the tip of Far Point a grasshopper warbler rose from the marrams in front of us and as it dived back into cover it fanned its broad, rounded tail. It had barely closed its wings before it began to run, looking remarkably like a small rodent as it scurried off through the low vegetation. It could climb over or under obstacles or weave through thick vegetation with equal speed and apparent ease. It then displayed its uncanny knack of vanishing before your eyes, never to be seen again.

The sky to the north was darkening rapidly and a sudden increase in the wind signalled that a further squall was imminent. We prepared ourselves for another soaking and just as the first drops of rain began to fall our attention was drawn to a tiny waif, purposefully flitting in our direction, low along one of the stony ridges. Its flitting flight took it past a whinchat and a pied flycatcher which were sheltering on the leeward side of some *Suaeda* bushes. As the rain intensified it took shelter close to us on the shingle against the gnarled trunk of one of the shrubby bushes. The dense foliage absorbed the wind and the rain leaving a neat half-moon of dry sand and shingle around the bird. Although it had fluffed up its feathers we could see that it had the broad white stripe over the eye and narrow white wing-bar of yet another greenish warbler!

The rain was becoming heavier so we made a hasty retreat to the dunes on Middle Point. While sheltering there amongst the long, spiky marram leaves we were able to rest and reflect on the events of the last two days. The chain of events seemed so incredible that it almost felt like a dream.

As the tail end of the squall headed inland over Morston the rain eased and the visibility improved. A long-winged gull-like bird could be seen coming up the channel. It was a skua but looked smaller and more delicately-built than an arctic skua and this impression was reinforced by its light and buoyant flight. As it came closer we could see that it had a pale head, lead-grey upperparts and a series of black-and-white 'zebra stripes' encircling its black tail. It was a young long-tailed skua and, instead of following the channel back to the sea, it decided to take a short cut and flew directly past us.

Whinchat

The departure of the skua low over the ridge and out to sea concluded two magical autumn days spent on Blakeney Point.

This fall of birds will long be remembered for the arrival of unprecedented numbers of greenish warblers. At least seven occurred on Blakeney Point alone and over thirty were found within the county. We had been privileged to have experienced one of those historic ornithological events and to have seen autumn migration on Blakeney Point at its most exciting.

Whitethroat

Greenish warbler sheltering from the rain

On a day of low cloud and drizzle fieldfares, redwings and a single ring ouzel pour out of the gloom and a woodcock rises from almost underfoot. The fine drizzle has left telltale marks in the watercolour washes.
The Plantation, 21st October 2000

This migrant long-eared was initially flushed from the dunes during the morning. It landed on a chestnut paling fence where it sat glaring back at me with its bright orange eyes. Here it roosted for the rest of the day allowing me the rare opportunity to make some sketches. Its velvety plumage was beautifully patterned with browns, greys, black and orange. I stayed watching it until dusk. Amazingly two short-eared owls appeared nearby before the long-eared suddenly became alert then flicked low over the beach and away over one of the ridges.
The Lupins, 12th November 2011

Seawatching

Little auks and dunlin moving along the breakers. Further out
kittiwakes, guillemots and a line of scoter battle against the storm.
Painted from the relative shelter of the beached fishing boats at Cley.
Northerly gale with rain and hail squalls, 12th November 2001

On Blakeney Point autumn is by far the best season for seawatching as this is when the highest number and variety of seabirds are migrating. Strong onshore winds, especially those from a northwesterly direction, provide the best conditions for witnessing large numbers of seabirds passing close inshore. Although the number and variety of birds may not rival those regularly recorded from the Atlantic-facing headlands of Cornwall and southwest Ireland, they can be spectacular and very exciting.

The most northerly section of the dunes is one of the best seawatching sites in Norfolk. Some years ago a hide was erected specifically for observing seabirds but unfortunately the dunes there are constantly being eroded and it was eventually deemed unsafe and was taken down. A series of replacements have been built from salvaged timber supplemented with tideline wreckage but in turn each hide has suffered the same fate and currently none remain.

Although some of the hides have appeared a little makeshift, they have provided the opportunity to see, in relative comfort, some rare species and spectacular seabird movements. They have, however, not been without their drawbacks as strong winds could blow sand from the eroded face of the dunes through the open viewing slats and into the eyes of the observers. More rarely, foam created by the pounding breakers has been forced up the beach by the tide and engulfed the hide. Such setbacks were a small price to pay for good views of seldom seen pelagic wanderers.

Pomarine skuas

Long-tailed skua

Onshore winds in late summer and early autumn can produce good movements of Manx shearwaters and there is always a chance of seeing an unusual bird, such as a storm petrel, a Balearic shearwater or even a rarity like a Cory's shearwater. At this time of year the first arctic skuas are regularly encountered and as the month progresses their numbers steadily increase. During strong onshore winds it is sometimes possible to pick out the spoon-ended tail of an adult pomarine skua or the impressive elongated streamers of a long-tailed skua.

The adult skuas are soon joined by increasing numbers of juveniles. Although arctic skuas are by far the most numerous it is, with experience, possible to pick out a young long-tailed or pomarine from their similar-looking cousin.

September is usually the best month to see the greatest variety of species. Great skuas or 'bonxies', kittiwakes, gannets and fulmars appear with increasing regularity. Small flocks of migrating waterfowl, predominantly teal, wigeon and common scoter, pass westwards and the first returning parties of brent geese start to appear.

When the weather is rough sooty shearwaters may be forced closer to the shore. Their darker underparts and powerful mechanical wing-action help distinguish them from the commoner black and white Manx shearwaters. During gales there is a real chance that a rarity, such as a Leach's petrel, Sabine's gull or grey phalarope could flash through at any moment and this exciting prospect helps observers to maintain concentration during the long hours of watching.

In October increasing numbers of razorbills, guillemots, divers, grebes and seaduck are to be seen passing offshore. Wigeon, teal and pintail are sometimes observed migrating in large numbers and, being gregarious birds, they often form large mixed flocks. From time to time dabbling ducks may join flocks of seaduck and some curious groupings can be seen. One of my favourite observations was of a tiny teal leading a line of big eider ducks with a couple of velvet scoters and wigeon thrown in for good measure and a young merganser tagging on behind!

Migrating wildfowl

Sooty shearwater and Leach's petrel

During November and early December it can be worthwhile dressing up warmly and enduring a few hours facing the bitterly cold northerly gales. Some of the winds originate in the arctic and can bring in some interesting northern specialities such as flocks of diminutive little auks. Little auks, although only starling-sized, are hardy birds and are usually quick to recover from being storm-blown. On the day following an arctic blast reorientating flocks of these charming birds can sometimes be seen moving westwards along the breakers.

Grey phalarope

A north-west gale had been blowing since first light. In the morning there were few signs of seabirds but by early afternoon large numbers of Manx shearwaters had started passing eastwards. The biggest flocks contained over a hundred birds and in total over a thousand were counted. Initially the shearwaters were quite distant but in the afternoon the tide had come in and many of them came close inshore. Here Manx shearwaters , a fulmar and two gannets pass eastwards whilst a lone sooty shearwater and a small flock of scoter head in the other direction.
Seawatching Hide, 29th August 2003

A Memorable Seawatch 10th September 2007

The preceding days had been dominated by a spell of warm, sunny weather and westerly winds. During the early hours of the 10th westerly gales originating in the mid-Atlantic were predicted to blow around the north of Scotland. At the same time a deep low pressure system was forecast to develop in the centre of the North Sea. This would draw the wind and any storm-driven seabirds into the southern North Sea.

In North Norfolk the wind was due to veer north-westerly then increase in strength around mid morning. These weather conditions were very unusual and promised to provide some exciting seawatching on the North Norfolk coast.

This excitement was all the greater for knowing that record numbers of great shearwaters had been seen off the Western Isles and a handful had even been seen in the North Sea as far south as

Sabine's gulls

Yorkshire. If the forecast held there now seemed to be a genuine prospect of one being seen off Norfolk and, for me personally, the opportunity of seeing a new species of seabird.

That morning I began watching from Cley but there was too much west in the wind and little in the way of seabird movement. So, after a while, I decided to wander up the Point towards the seawatching hide.

By ten o'clock I had reached the Hood and had the seawatching hide firmly in my sights. In an instant the wind veered sharply to the north-west and increased in strength. The sea began to roughen and large numbers of seabirds were suddenly moving past and at all ranges. It was an extraordinary transformation. A huge circling mass of birds was visible on the north-western horizon which, when viewed through binoculars, was seen to be a cloud of hundreds of spiralling gannets. The spectacle was incredibly exciting and one which I had never before experienced off the Norfolk coast.

Bonxies, fulmars, little gulls and even more gannets now streamed eastwards; it was just as if a tap had been turned on! A chain of eight dark, lithe birds suddenly broke the skyline; it was a group of sooty shearwaters passing by at close range. I quickened my step and on reaching the foot of the dunes that lead up to the hide I found two of

Great and sooty shearwaters

Great shearwater

the wardens hunkered down in one of the hollows. They had tried watching from the hide but, as soon as the slats were opened, clouds of sand had been blown into their faces. The only option was to crouch down in the dunes to try and gain some shelter from the wind.

The birds continued to stream by with fulmars, gannets and little gulls being the most numerous but there were also good numbers of bonxies and sooty shearwaters. They were passing by at all distances, ranging from just behind the crashing breakers to as far as the horizon and it was difficult to know where to look.

Just before midday my attention was drawn to a seabird moving eastwards in the company of two sooty shearwaters. It too was a shearwater but it looked slightly heavier in build and paler-grey brown above than its companions. As it banked I caught sight of a white collar and a dark cap. I could scarcely believe my eyes for it was my first ever great shearwater! Although there had seemed a possibility that one would reach Norfolk I never really believed that I would see one. Later in the day two more passed by, at even closer range, and I was able to see clearly the distinctive dark markings on their otherwise

gleaming white underparts. Further along the coast at Sheringham observers, watching from the comfort of the shelters on the seafront, logged the incredible tally of fifteen great shearwaters. These were the first to be seen in Norfolk for ten years and the count exceeded the all time county total!

From the dunes on Blakeney Point other unusual seabirds were also seen moving through. Two Leach's petrels passed by in their characteristic manner. They zigzagged through the wave troughs with powerful, elastic wing-beats. Their flight was fast and sometimes hard to follow as they made frequently erratic changes of direction. Other highlights included four Sabine's gulls en route from their arctic breeding grounds to their tropical Atlantic winter quarters. Initially two separate juveniles passed westwards along the surf to be followed by another youngster accompanied by a stunning summer-plumaged adult.

The variety of species and the sheer number of birds passing through made the hours race by. That evening, as I walked back along the ridge to Cley, I came to realise just how fortunate I had been to witness such an extraordinary event. Naturally I was thrilled to have seen a new species of bird but my mind kept returning to the moment when the wind swung to the north-west and then increased in strength. To have witnessed the seascape suddenly transformed to one of a boiling mass of birds is my overriding memory of that exciting day.

Little gulls and bonxies

A juvenile long-tailed skua 'dip-feeding' and a fulmar
disappearing from sight in a wave trough.
Cley Beach, northwesterly gale, 4th September 2001

Dark juvenile

Pale juvenile

Long-tailed Skuas

The north-facing coast of Norfolk is a good location, during onshore gales, to see this rare seabird. The majority of sightings are of juvenile birds and some experience is required in order to pick them out from the very similar arctic and pomarine skuas. To complicate matters the juveniles occur in various plumages from dark to pale. With practice it is possible to identify this exciting bird using a combination of size, structure and plumage characteristics.

Two medium phase juveniles behind a juvenile arctic skua

Storm-driven little auks. Although regarded as one of the world's most numerous, birds these starling-sized birds are only occasionally seen off Blakeney Point during late autumn gales. This painting, in common with several others of seabirds, was completed while sheltering behind beached fishing boats near Cley Beach. On such occasions it is as much a challenge to keep hold of the paper and mixing palette as it is to complete the painting. Northerly gale, 14th November 2001

These little auks had only just paused to rest on the sea
when a young herring gull appeared and caused them to
take flight again. During gales the opportunistic large gulls
are always on the lookout for weary seabirds and a tired
little auk would be an easy target for these powerful birds.
Cley, 12th November 2001

Grey Seals Pupping

Cows with three or four day-old pups.
Far Point, 16th November 2011

On my first day as a warden on Blakeney Point I became aware of unfamiliar melodic cries emanating from Far Point. They sounded almost human and had a mournful, song-like quality but I soon realised that these were the voices of grey seals. Their 'songs' were to become familiar to me during that first season. They carried especially well on still days and on calm nights I could even hear them calling from the harbour as I lay in bed in the Lifeboat House.

At that time, the mid 1990s, grey seals were the less common of the two species of seal found on the Point but counts of 200 to 300 were sometimes made during the summer months. The first instance of a grey seal giving birth on Blakeney Point was recorded in 1988. During the following decade there were occasional records of pups being seen in late autumn or early winter. At the end of 2001 about twenty-five pups were born there and this event marked the beginning of an established breeding colony or 'rookery'. In subsequent years there has been a staggering rise in the number of pups being born and in 2011 a record 933 pups were counted.

The pattern of peak pupping periods around the coast of the British Isles follows an interesting pattern. In Cornwall and the Isles of Scilly most pups are born in August and September but, moving clockwise around the coastline, the young are born increasingly later. The peak pupping period on Blakeney Point lasts from late November to mid December and these pups are amongst the latest to be born in Britain.

Pup suckling

In 2011 I had the opportunity to spend some time on the Point observing and painting the fascinating life of the grey seal rookery there. The first pup of the season was seen on 28th October. A dozen pups were present by 6th November and by the 20th the number of young had increased to 376. On 7th December a count of 775 was made and by the end of the month 932 pups had been recorded. On 24th January 2012 the warden unexpectedly found a pup which was only a few days old and this exceptionally late birth took the season's total to 933.

The following section describes the breeding cycle of grey seals and included in the text are entries from my 2011 diaries. I hope that these extracts will help to further illustrate the behaviour of the seals from the formation of the rookery in early autumn to the start of the New Year when the seals begin to disperse.

During the second half of October increasing numbers of adult grey seals are to be seen at the haul-out sites. Many of the females are heavily pregnant and the majority of bulls are in peak breeding condition and look exceptionally powerful. Whereas it takes bulls six years to reach sexual maturity, the females can reach breeding age when they are between three and five years old.

Newborn pup

Bull, cow and pup

The bulls are quick to stake claim to a section of the beach or dunes for themselves and then fiercely defend it from other males. Fights often ensue, which result in the establishment of a hierarchy. Only the more dominant bulls will attract a harem of females. The bulls guard the females until their pups are weaned and they are ready to mate.

5th November 2011

Many bulls are actively defending territories on the seaward side of Far Point. Lots of cows have begun to come ashore there and at least five pups are visible. On the landward side of Far Point the first bulls have just started to move onto the ridges and venture towards the dunes but no cows are yet present in these areas.

6th November 2011

Suddenly lots of bulls have begun moving into the dunes around Far Point and there have been many instances of threatening behaviour and some fighting between bulls. The first groups of cows have also started to arrive there. One cow had already given birth. The newborn pup was typically thin-looking with its creamy pelt appearing too big for its bony body. A long length of umbilical cord was still attached. There was a bit of fresh blood on its fur and the placenta lay close by.

7th November 2011

Bulls are seemingly everywhere now and lots more cows moving into the dunes, some even moving up onto the main dune ridge. Hundreds of adult seals now present on the beach side, their numbers have at least trebled during the last three days. At least fifteen pups could be seen on Far Point.

8th November 2011

Lots more pups today with at least thirty-five visible on the end of Far Point.

The pups are born in their white 'baby' coats. At birth this 'lanugo' is frequently a bright buttery colour having been stained by the yellowy amniotic fluid of the placental bag. The buttery coloration remains on the fur until it is washed away by rain or saltwater. However, the young, if left undisturbed, will usually stay out of the sea for the first month or so of their lives. The pups soon begin to shed their pale fur and the first signs of moult are visible after only a few days. The mottled grey adult-like coat begins to show first on the pup's nose, face and hind flippers and after four weeks the pale 'baby' coat will have gone completely.

13th November 2011

A quick count revealed at least 155 pups around Far Point. Many pups actively suckling. Lots of instances of bulls fighting; most fights involved bulls that had challenged existing males for possession of their territories. The victorious bulls would chase the rivals out of their territories which could sometimes wreak havoc amongst the

Mother and pup fast asleep

14 Nov 11 Far Point

The bull guards the females in his harem from the attentions of
other males. Under his protection the females will give birth and
raise their young. Only when the pups are weaned will the
females be ready to mate. 14th November 2011

mothers and pups. One cow was watched lying next to her pup that had been injured and subsequently died. The bond between mother and her dead pup was very strong and remained so for several days. It was very moving to see her continually nudging the pup with her nose as if trying to make it respond. Many of the youngest pups regularly called to their mothers and the sound was sometimes remarkably similar to that of a human baby or at other times reminiscent of the bleating of a newborn lamb.

It was quite a powerful experience to continually witness at close quarters the extremes of behaviour at the rookery; from the frequent violent and bloody clashes between the bulls to the tenderness and maternal care that the cows showed for their newborn pups. Having recently become a father I found the behaviour especially fascinating and, at times, surprisingly emotional.

Several of the dominant bulls regularly made loud, slapping noises by 'belly-flopping' on wet sand and in shallow water. This behaviour was often used as a threat towards rival males but may have had a dual function as a show of dominance to their cows.

As soon as the pups begin to suckle they fill out rapidly and start to develop at a surprising rate. The female's milk is at least 50% fat and is said to be ten times richer than even Jersey cows' milk. The pups are weaned after only three weeks. However, producing such rich milk puts a tremendous strain on the fasting mothers and towards the end of lactation period many cows become visibly thin. Once the pups are weaned the mothers head out to sea to feed.

A pup beginning to show signs of moult

Ovulation occurs towards the end of the weaning period and it is only then that the bull has his chance to mate with each cow in his highly-defended harem.

Bulls fighting

The grey seal has the same remarkable breeding cycle as that of the common seal. The cows, whilst fasting, will have lost around a quarter of their body weight so are not in good enough physical condition to become pregnant straight away.

After mating the fertilised embryo does not immediately attach to the wall of the uterus but instead floats free in a dormant state for around three and a half months. By this stage the cow will have regained her body weight and will then be ready for the beginning of eight months of pregnancy. This arrested development of the embryo also ensures that the pups are born at the same time each year and the grey seal's annual cycle is preserved.

19th November 2011
Over 350 pups today. Many becoming really big and some weaned pups appearing almost balloon-like! Many of their white coats showing signs of active moult and some of the dark spots of their first adult coat are visible between the thinning white fur.

Several cows have started showing signs of affection towards bulls, especially after a bull had successfully seen off a rival. The first instance of mating recorded today.

Lots of fighting between bulls noted. Most, if not all, conflicts, seem to be caused by bulls entering into already established territories and on every occasion that was observed the challenging male lost the fight. Some of the fights were very violent and several bulls exhibited large gashes and blood-stained heads and necks.

Some of the defeated bulls were driven out of one territory only to find themselves in the middle of another one where they would be attacked instantly. One poor bull was exhausted from repeated attacks, having become trapped in the middle of five adjoining territories. He had several open wounds and would move away from attacking bulls by rolling along the sand. This vulnerable-looking posture appeared to be a show of submission. On occasions it seemed to work but it didn't always guarantee him a safe passage.

In other fights I also noticed that other defeated bulls would break off a fight by using this rolling behaviour. Some of the bulls that had large open wounds and big patches of fur matted with dried blood and sand looked quite repulsive. During some of the most prolonged violent encounters many cows were forced to move out of the way. Pups were less inclined, or less able, to move and appeared to be in real danger of being crushed. Many cows are very protective of their pups and will readily threaten and even attack bulls that venture too close to their young.

On the seaward side of the Point the colony had spread to nearly half a mile in length.

6th December 2011

Over 650 pups were visible today. Lots of the older pups were in heavy moult and where they have been lying in the dunes the sand and marrams are covered with fine white hairs. Small 'puffs' of fur could be seen drifting in the wind. Many of the cows with pups close to weaning were beginning to look very thin. Although there was a westerly gale blowing today the weather was crisp and sunny and it was a fantastic sight seeing all the seals lined up along the beach with a raging sea behind them. Lots of sand was being blown over the beach and had started to cover some of the pups. They seemed totally unfazed by this and remained asleep. Although the colony looked stunning on the seaward side the conditions were too harsh for painting so I opted to do some sketching in the sheltered dunes.

10th December 2011

The majority of the pups looked to have been weaned. They had clearly been very well fed and many looked fit to burst! Most of the bigger pups had finished moulting and many of the rest had just isolated patches of white fur left on their backs. Some had left their favoured loafing areas and the only signs remaining of the pups were flattened marram grass and moulted fur. Many of the independent pups had moved low down on the beach and a few were seen swimming in the open sea as far down the Point as Cley beach. A couple of small groups of adolescent pups were hanging around the tidal sands. One gang of eight pups bounded in tight formation towards the breakers as I walked back along the beach.

There were lots of instances of courtship and mating between the adults seals. A few newborn pups could be seen but there were increasing signs that the pupping season was drawing to a close and the rookery beginning to break up.

It will be interesting to follow the fortunes of this rapidly expanding rookery. Its establishment and the explosive nature of its growth in little over a decade is a further example of the constantly evolving natural history of this remarkable place.

Bull fast asleep

Bull, cow and suckling pup.   20th November 2011

Bull, cow and pup. 20th November 2011

Grey Seal Pups

The pups are born with a full coat of pale fur. They look exceedingly attractive in this first or 'baby' coat but within just a few days they begin to moult. By the time the pups are two weeks old many show large patches on their faces, heads and flippers where the pale fur has been shed to reveal the adult-like coat below. After three weeks much of the pale fur has gone but the pups will still have some patches remaining on their backs. When the pups are four weeks old they will have moulted completely.

At birth the young look very thin but after their first few feeds they rapidly begin to fill out. Seal milk is extremely rich and the young develop amazingly quickly. The young are weaned after only three weeks and by this stage they will have over trebled their birth weight and many appear almost balloon-like. The young, now independent, will need these fat reserves as they will soon take to the sea and learn to fend for themselves.

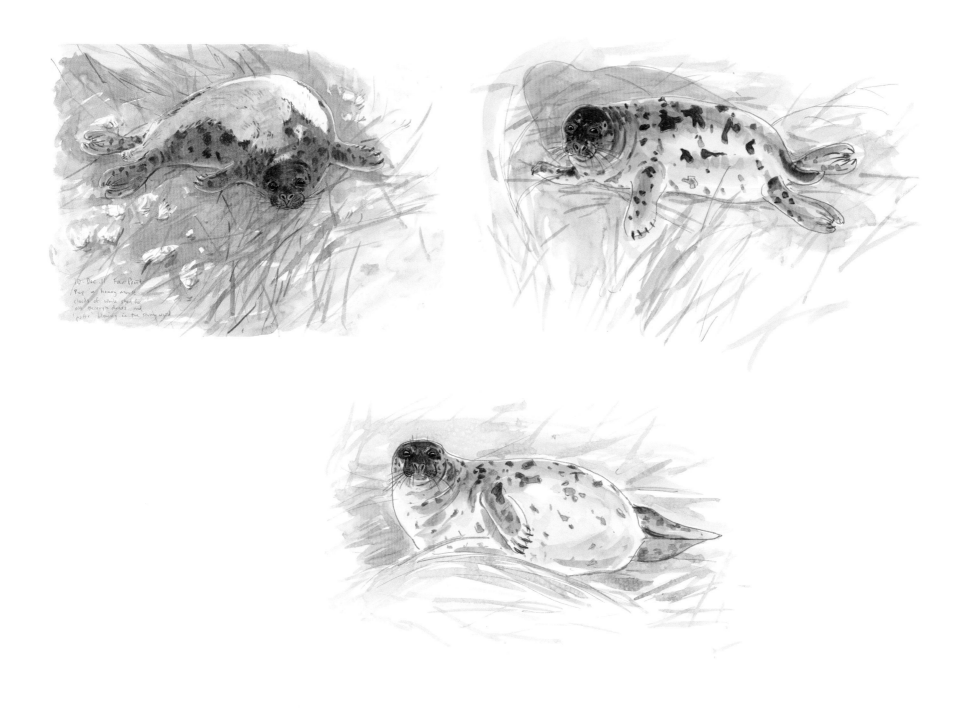

10 Dec 11 Far Point
Pup in heavy moult
clouds of white shed fur
all through dunes and
spatter blowing in the strong wind

147

The cows and pups show much affection
and tenderness towards each other. In great
contrast many bulls show scars from violent
conflicts with their rivals.
10th December 2011

Dozing bull amid his harem. Only when the pups are
weaned do the cows begin to ovulate and give the bull the
opportunity to mate. Until then he will fiercely defend
his area of beach from any trespassing males. Bright but
cold, strong west wind, Far Point, 6th December 2011

Winter

Four inches of snow had fallen during the night but by mid morning
the temperature had risen to above freezing and the snow began to
thaw. By the afternoon the only snow remaining was to be found on
the shaded, north-facing storm ridges. A lone hare, disturbed from its
daytime resting place, flees along one of the long bands of snow.
The Watch House, 6th February 2012

Midwinter is the quietest period for wildlife on Blakeney Point. The bustling activity of the grey seal colony begins to wane after Christmas. The landscape seems bleak and exposed to the elements and harsh weather conditions make it seem more open and remote than in other seasons. During winter storms it is a truly wild place but it can be beautiful and extremely peaceful on bright, crisp and still days.

Shorelarks

A few dunnocks, wrens, reed buntings and skylarks may stay to eke out a living beneath the *Suaeda* bushes or at the edge of the saltings but the majority have dispersed in search of richer pickings. Some hardy species, however, choose this remote landscape for their winter home. Rock pipits exchange the wave-pounded rocky shores and sea cliffs of Scandinavia for the relative warmth and shelter of the saltmarsh creeks.

Snow buntings abandon the snow and ice of their upland breeding areas to pick through the tideline debris or search for seeds along the open beaches. Occasionally they are joined by a few Lapland buntings and sometimes a small flock of shorelarks can be seen feeding amongst the withered samphire plants.

The presence of small birds attracts regular visits from wintering merlins. These are most often seen flashing by, low over the shingle, or sitting on a driftwood vantage point watching out for potential prey.

Away from the noise of the open sea and the crunch of shingle underfoot the dunes can become eerily quiet. Without the voices of breeding larks and pipits the landscape seems strangely unfamiliar. It is only when a hare rises from its form amongst the marrams or a short-eared owl from its daytime roost that the mood is broken.

The open sea and harbour tend to hold more signs of life. A scan along the breakers may show a few red-throated divers, great crested grebes or guillemots fishing offshore. In the shelter of the harbour small numbers of mergansers, goldeneyes and little grebes can be found in the creeks and channels. A more thorough search may produce scarcer species such as a striking black and white Slavonian grebe or an impressive cormorant-sized great northern diver.

Slavonian grebe

Flocks of brent geese regularly interrupt their feeding on the coastal grassland and fly into the harbour to wash and drink. They also roost there and at dawn and dusk their lovely muttering calls can be heard as they take flight.

Red-throated divers

Little grebes

Peregrine

The food-rich sandflats and mudflats continue to attract to wading birds. Curlews, godwits, oystercatchers, grey plovers, redshanks, dunlins and turnstones favour the harbour while sanderlings prefer the open sandy shores where they dash along the edge of the surf. Small groups of teal, wigeon, pintail and a few mallard gather to feed amongst the old samphire beds and at dusk their numbers are swollen when others flight in to join them.

From time to time the wildfowl and waders will rise in a sudden panic. The appearance of a lithe, powerful peregrine is frequently the cause of all the commotion as it tries to single out a victim from the swirling flocks.

Young glaucous gull

The weather is usually at it coldest in the second half of the winter and the open landscape provides little shelter from the elements. The presence of a large biscuit-coloured glaucous gull resting on the open beach indicates that the bitter winds are of arctic origin.

Despite the cold temperatures the lengthening daylight hours hint that the end of winter is slowly approaching. It will not be too long before the first calls of Sandwich terns herald the arrival of spring and the beginning of a new chapter in the history of Blakeney Point.

The Watch House in the snow. 6th February 2012

Snow and Lapland buntings search amongst the shingle for seeds.
20th December 2007

Brent geese, a grey plover and a turnstone feeding in the harbour.
Bright but very cold, late afternoon, 10th November 2001

At dusk brent geese that have spent the day feeding
on the grazing marshes between Cley and Salthouse,
flight into Blakeney harbour to roost.
Cold, crisp and still, February 2012

This book is dedicated to all who have a love of this wild and beautiful place and to the memory of Janet Reed, John Bean, Tim Lubbock and Simon Aspinall.

Acknowledgements

I am most grateful to Richard Porter for writing the foreword. Richard is a well-known and respected figure in the world of ornithology not least for his work in the Middle East. His very first visit to Blakeney Point was on the 5th April 1959. In 1999 he came to live in Cley and soon adopted the Point as his 'local patch'. He now spends much of his spare time there studying the flora and fauna.

Many thanks also to David Wood for providing 'Blakeney Point Beginnings'. Producing a short, concise summary of a place with so much history is no mean feat and I'm very pleased to be able to include this historical chapter.

To Joe Reed for sharing some of his experience of the lives of the Point's breeding birds. His knowledge, especially during my first summer as a seasonal warden, helped me to understand more clearly the ways of nesting birds and fuelled my growing interest in the behaviour of wildlife. This interest still remains and has become one of the main focuses of my artwork.

To the National Trust wardens, some of whom have gone on to become good friends. This is especially true of David Wood and Aaron Boughtflower, with whom I spent a really enjoyable season in 2003, and the current long-serving wardens, Ed Stubbings and Paul Nichols, for their hospitality and good company. Many thanks also to the other National Trust staff, including John Sizer and Graham Lubbock, for their help over the years.

I would also like to thank David Wood, Aaron Boughtflower, Ed Stubbings, Paul Nichols, Richard Porter, Andy Stoddart, Steve Joyner, Giles Dunmore, Chris Wheeler, Tony Marr and the numerous other observers in whose company I have spent many enjoyable days watching migrant birds.

To the ferrymen for their regular lifts to the Point during my time spent there as a warden.

To John Walters for his continued help and enthusiasm in both my work and the production of the books. His design skills have again transformed my rough mock-up into beautifully designed pages.

In a similar vein Roger and Margot Brownsword have kindly devoted much time to helping me ensure that the text is clear and precise. This skill is especially useful when trying to explain clearly some of the complicated behavioural sequences of the breeding birds. The final versions of what are ultimately short paragraphs often took many hours of lively discussion.

Many thanks to Andy Stoddart for casting his eye over various versions of the text and commenting on the grammar and punctuation.

Finally to my partner, Natasha and our daughter, Nola for all their love, understanding and support particularly during my continued long days spent on Blakeney Point "collecting reference material".

Bibliography and Further Reading

The Birds of Blakeney Point, Stoddart, A. and Joyner, S. 2005, Wren Publishing.

Notes on the Birds of Cley, Pashley, H.N. 1925, H.F. & G. Witherby, London.

Bird Sanctuary, Gaze, R. 1947, Faber & Faber Ltd.

Birds of Norfolk, Taylor, M. et al. 1999, Pica Press.

Blakeney Point and Scolt Head Island, Allison, H. & Morley, J.P. 1989, The National Trust.

Sea Swallows, Pinchen, R.J. 1935.

Countryman's Memoirs – A Warden's Life on Blakeney Point, Eales, W. J. 1986, Privately published.

Waders their Breeding, Haunts and Watchers, Nethersole-Thompson D & M. 1886, T. & A. D. Poyser.

Grey Seal, Common Seal, Survival Book No.6, Lockley R. M. 1966, Andre Deutsch Ltd.

The Birds of the Western Palearctic, Volumes 1-9, Cramp, S. et al, 1977-1994, Oxford University Press.

Moulted shell of the swimming crab *Liocarcinus holsatus*

tracks in snow
6·2·12 Watch House

2 Dec 11
Far Point

cold + windy